WE ACCEPT HER, ONE OF US

WE ACCEPT HER, ONE OF US

DIANE GOLDIE

Art Credits

COVER ART BY DIANE GOLDIE (SELF PORTRAIT AS TARGET, 2024)

ILLUSTRATIONS BY DIANE GOLDIE AND IMOGEN GOLDIE

We Accept Her, One of Us

AN EXPLORATION OF WOMANHOOD, FROM JEZEBEL TO CRONE QUEEN

DIANE GOLDIE

Contents

Art Credits	iii
We Accept Her, One of Us	iv
Dedication	x
Foreward	xi
Part 1 How The Light Got In	1
1 Keep the Fires Burning	7
2 The Elderflower Tree	11
3 Who is Imogen?	15
Part 2 Little Diane in Kansas	23
4 Mum's early years	25
5 The Ballad of Uncle Stephen	28
6 It's Normal to Kiss Strangers	32
7 My Relationship with Fairies	34
8 A Scruffy Fairy Alter Ego and a Symbolic Tattoo	35
9 The Grecian Dress and Infidelity	41
10 Mum, Me and the Roses	43
11 Make Believe Play	45
12 Early music influences	47
13 Pets, Nature and Wales	49

14 Drawing Dougal 52
15 Nan through my eyes 54
16 Early Education 56
17 Clifford and the Valentine's card 61
18 First Boys Party 63
19 Social Struggles and my First Period 66
20 Uncle Stephen and the Secret 69
21 Strikes, Candlelit Baths, DDT & Teasing Witches 71
22 Porn, Santa, & the Man in the Window 73
23 Leaving On a Jet Plane 75

Part 3 Munchkinland 80

24 An English Girl in Africa 82
25 Important Decisions and New Discoveries 88
26 The Body Holds on to Unkind Words 92
27 You say Goodbye, I say Hello! 95

Part 4 A Story Within a Story 98

28 How Not to Get Raped 111
29 Chinese Party and the Pain. 116
30 Jan's First Voice Note 119
31 Fourteen year old journal entry 121
32 Jan's Second Voice Note 122
33 Dear Diary, It's Me Again 125
34 Conversation with Jan, Aged 64 129
35 Boundaries 133
36 An Open Letter to Jan 137

Part 5 Jezebel 139

37 Come Sit Here For A While, Little Diane 142

38	Vampire at Christian Camp	144
39	Lion, meet Scarecrow	146
40	A Saved Jezebel	148
41	Makeovers and Confirmation Fraud	149
42	The Dowlings and Losing Jesus	152
43	Craig	154
44	I've Been Told That You've Been Bold	156
45	Out of the Frying Pan into the Fire	161
46	The Green House & The Wild Bird	166
47	You Shall Go to the Ball	170
48	Jesus Wants YOU!	180
49	An Angel called Sam	185
50	Cosplaying Myself	189
Part 6	There's No Place Like Home	195
51	The God Lie	207
52	Marriage, Motherhood and Me	210
53	Millennium	219
54	Dance	229
55	My Divided Self Emerges	239
56	Sacred & Profane	242
57	Reflections of Me	254
58	Finding My Voice	282
59	I Am An Artist	284
60	Little Dead Wren and the Rollercoaster	289
61	The Final Artwork	295
62	A Conversation with a former Skeptic	301
63	On Being a Grandma	309
64	Home	317

VIII ~ WE ACCEPT HER, ONE OF US

65 On Menopause and Ageing   321

Afterward   328
About the Author   330

Copyright © 2025 by Diane Goldie
All rights reserved. No part of this book may be reproduced in any manner whatsoever without written permission except in the case of brief quotations embodied in critical articles and reviews.
First Printing, 2025

This book is dedicated to Imogen and all those women and girls who lost their way thinking they were broken and left too soon, and Allegra, for the showing me the way forward.

Foreward

Is it oversharing?

Or just authentic communication about things that really matter?

I think it is time for a reframe.

Small talk has never made sense to me.

Are you ready for some big talk?

Part 1 How The Light Got In

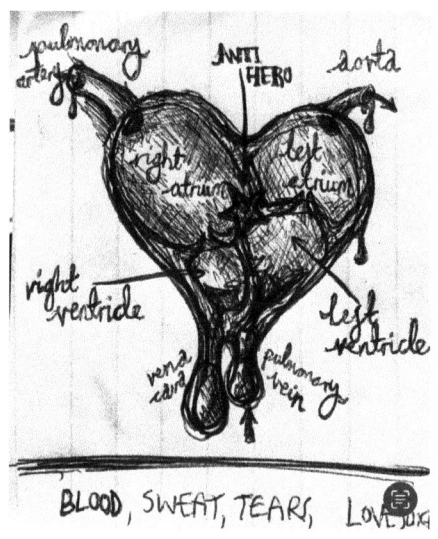

The quiet, cosy after-dinner atmosphere was disturbed by an ominous knock on the front door. I turned to my long term partner and quizzically raised an eyebrow. Was he expecting visitors on this quiet New Year's Day evening? I certainly wasn't. The social season was officially done for a while and I was relieved. As much as I enjoyed gatherings with friends and family, my relief on restoring quiet solitude was evident.

Knock! Knock!

I opened the front door and my heart sank. My deepest, darkest fear was about to manifest. I knew why those two female police officers were here.

"Diane Goldie?"

"Yes, she's dead isn't she? "

"Can we come in?"

For the next few moments, time seemed to warp, stretch out and slow down. The air seemed to turn to dense fog as I grappled to deal with the shock of the officers telling me that my daughter had killed herself out in Cambodia the previous day. The previous day had been her 28th birthday. December 31st 2016 would be forever remembered as the day my heart cracked open and I was forced to surrender to what is, from that moment onwards. My life, and the life of my little family would never be the same again.

I'd read that people grieve differently, and I'd seen plenty of true crime dramas where I'd seen families receive similar news. I wondered if I was responding appropriately to the officers. Was I supposed to scream, cry or faint? Instead I had felt the deepest empathy for these two women forced to deliver the worst news to a mother as part of their everyday job. I wondered how they could do this job on a daily basis, how did they cope? My mind raced with these thoughts and I blurted out,

"Can I give you a hug?"

I noticed the obvious discomfort spreading over their faces and wondered if I'd done it wrong again, but they allowed me to hug them despite the awkwardness now flooding the narrow hallway. My emotions seemed far away on some other distant dimension as did my body. Was I dreaming? I snapped back into my body and realised I hadn't asked about Imogen's love, Rob.

"There was someone else there, wasn't there?"

"Yes, a man"

"Was it her husband? Is he dead also?"

" We can't confirm that officially but do you have contact details for his family?"

I did, and dutifully passed them on.

Within the week, my youngest daughter and I were on a flight out to Cambodia to cremate Imogen's remains and to bring back her few possessions plus her ashes in an ornate bronze urn. She had left a suicide note requesting her ashes to be scattered in the sea at the beach where she had her most happy childhood memories, Wells-Next-The-Sea. It didn't escape me that my baby had married on Christmas day on an island off of Sihanoukville, becoming Imogen Goldie-Wells.

As funerals go, Imogen couldn't have planned a more fitting one for herself. Buddhist monks chanted in their saffron robes as incense burned at the outdoor cremation temple. Butterflies fluttered around us in the warm, fragrant air. I was even asked if I wanted to press the button that would incinerate her. Apparently it is a beautiful part of the local custom to do that. It felt right. A bit like cutting the cord at birth, but in reverse. This funeral was far superior to any stuffy Church service I'd ever attended back home in the UK.

In the midst of the general hysteria that comes as part of the grieving process, pushing through the shock and tears like a Tim Burton Jack-in-a-box, was a moment of pure hilarity. As our taxi approached the temple cremation site, my daughter and I could see Imo-

gen's wooden coffin up ahead covered with dramatic floral displays of bright white waxy flowers. As we pulled closer, both of us burst out laughing as we simultaneously heard Imogen's irritated voice in our heads, shouting :

"What the Fuck!"

A twice life size blow up of her passport photo was hanging off of the end of the coffin. We both knew just how much Imogen would have been visually offended by this and we weren't at all surprised to hear her objection, albeit of the spirit variety.

It may be considered weird to some, but hearing spirit and other paranormal occurrences was just part of our family's everyday normal. I'd never really given it much thought. I'd said something about this in passing to my maternal cousin who confirmed it was very much a family 'gift' thing, possibly to do with our Romany heritage on maternal line of the family. My mum's mum, (Nan) would often speak about my great-great-grandma being burned in her caravan when she died. I've never validated this claim but it remains a fond family legend. My nan, with her olive skin, jet black dead straight hair, buxom bosom and bright green eyes was the very picture of the romanticized Roma woman.

My nan

It was a pity she was born in a time when a flat chest, wavy blond hair and pale skin was the height of fashion. We've always been outsiders, it seems, and I'm very proud of our differences, now that I am aware that we are different, that is. For the longest time I just presumed everyone was just like us, and that the world was just broken and that is why we struggled, because everyone struggles, right? This way of thinking formed the basis of how I missed Imogen's autism for so long. Imogen had killed herself because she thought she was broken. Living by neurotypical standards and expectations had been at the root of her deep pain that she had expressed from a small child, starting with terrifying night terrors that she regularly would struggle with from the age of four.

Losing my child was the darkest point of my life. My heart cracked open but the Kintsugi-like gold repair was uncovering our family's neurodivergence.

There is a crack, a crack in everything. It's how the light gets in.

Thank you for that lyric, Leonard. It got me through the darkest of days.
Thank you Imogen for showing us all our true nature.

1

Keep the Fires Burning

Jan 2025

It's cold outside, minus three or something equally bone chilling, but I'm cosy here inside.

I've decided to light a real fire inside in my grate and for two days now I've managed to tend to it and keep the embers glowing throughout the night.

There's nothing more grounding than sitting in front of a real fire, watching the flickering flames and staring deep into the orange bellied glow of the embers. In this modern age of central heating, we've been robbed of this mundane, yet profound ritual of connection to the ancestors. I've decided to bring it back, albeit in my home with smoke free fuel.

For some years now I've been listening and responding to a deeper call. A decade ago, I became aware of a sense of urgency and a need to prepare people for something up ahead. What it was, I didn't know, but I knew it was going to be impactful. I created a capsule collection of wearable art that bore phrases such as URGENT! or IT'S TIME! or ARE YOU READY? in big, bold letters on punky, chunky clothing.

I was quite taken aback at how positively they were received and the collection sold out immediately.

The following year, Imogen died and I rationalised that it was her death that I had been sensing, but now I sit here and stare at the flames in my fireplace as over in the USA, swathes of Hollywood burns, I'm not sure.

There's definitely something in the air this year and spirit is whispering to me that everyone is about to find out what. All I know for certain is that everything needs to change, and for real change to happen, everything needs to be broken down beyond the point of repair. This feels like our collective Tower moment.

The tower tarot card depicts a tower being struck by lightning as people fall from it to their certain deaths below. This signifies a radical, unforeseen change. I believe we need to start again with a new system, a new fairer way that works with, not against, our planet. After all, we have moved into a new age of Aquarius (when Pluto transits into the sign of Aquarius). The last few times our planet was under the influence of this transit, we had the French, American and Haitian revolutions and US civil rights protests. Maybe this is all just New Age nonsense, maybe I'm just being another street preacher doom-monger evangelist or Eat Less Protein guy with his placard, perhaps we've always believed our times to be the worst, but things certainly feel far more chaotic now than they did when I was. a child half a century ago. I'm ready for things to fall apart. Let it come.

As a child who grew up in the cold East Midlands, in a house with no central heating, lighting the family fire was my regular daily chore. I'd wake up to intricate fractal frost patterns on the inside of the windows, and with visible breath amusing me as if I was smoking an invisible cigarette, I'd head downstairs and set the fire in the living room to heat our home.

Making fire should be a basic skill every human should acquire. It's a step by step process. Paper twists, twigs or wood kindling are placed in a teepee formation, then larger pieces of wood over the top, making sure to keep adequate air flow. Coal or logs are placed last once the fire is established. To get a good draw of air to really fuel the fire, a large sheet of newspaper is held taught across the fireplace opening, creating an updraught of air in the chimney. It is a bit like magic, and remains a thrillingly dangerous exercise, especially for a child as the paper can potentially ignite and get sucked up the chimney if it isn't held taught enough across the fireplace opening. In the late 60's and 70's we took far more risks as children. This current generation of children have been robbed of these basic soul-feeding things in the age of virtual reality, fast food and central heating. There's so much to be gained from the basic things.

My nine-year-old grandson recently sat mesmerised for hours in front of my open fire, strangely still and calm, cheeks glowing and eyes sparkling. I'm so used to seeing him bouncing off of the walls, making vocal tics and complaining of being bored if there wasn't a screen to watch. It was remarkable to see him like this, transfixed by this simple yet unusual event of indoor fire. He asked me to invite him around the very next time I decided to make a fire again as it was his new favourite thing.

We all need to come together once again, like our ancestors, and sit around our fires, staring into stillness and wonder, deep into the radiant embers of the mystery recalling our deep knowings. Do not believe the talk of short attention spans in our youngsters, they've just not been given the opportunity and space to stand and stare. In our transactional society, the power found in stillness for stillness's sake, has been forgotten.

As a child on Bonfire night, my favourite part wasn't the loud, visual spectacle that was the firework display. They filled my heart with awe and wonder, (once my nervous system had recovered from the shock of the sudden bangs) but my whole being felt at home when I stood in front of a giant bonfire shoulder to shoulder with the rest of the local community. Standing around a large fire as a group, feeling the heat of the flames scorching our freezing cheeks, seemed so familiar, so right.

Once during the trance state found in dancing the rhythm of chaos in my 5 Rhythms dance practice, I felt as if I was dancing around a giant bonfire outside even though I was indoors in a sports hall. Ancestral memory and knowing came dancing through the ether. It reminded me of exactly who I was and who was standing behind me with their hands on my shoulders and with hands on their shoulders, going far back into the mists of time.

I realised Imogen was now the first female ancestor standing behind me with her hands on my shoulders being my most recent ancestor, and that moment felt poignant and pure. Even though she was younger than I in body, I knew that her spirit had always been destined to be my teacher.

2

The Elderflower Tree

I know it's a cliche but I've become a tree hugger. This transpired after a tree spoke to me. Let me tell you how I got to that weird place. I'd been drinking lots of elderflower cordial, not only because it was delicious, but it was also one of the very few dilutables that had nothing chemical or nasty in it. I'm unable to drink water on its own because to me it tastes like death or plastic, so I need to flavour it to disguise the horrible taste. Elderflower cordial is made simply by steeping elderflowers in a sugar syrup. What am I going on about and what does this have to do with trees talking to me, you may ask? There is a theory starting to form here, but first let me tell you about the tree reaching out to me.

I was on my usual dog walk in the fairly grubby local park, and a storm broke. Sheltering under trees during electrical storms is probably not ideal, but I figured if I picked a short, bushy tree, my chances of being fried by a bolt of lightning would be minimal. I needed shelter from the rain, it was coming down sideways and my kimono was certainly no match for the weather. I dashed for shelter under the closest, scrubbiest tree directly next to the dog poo bin (glamorous it certainly wasn't) standing as near to the trunk as I could to maximise shelter. It was then that I heard it.

"Hold me!"

I spun around to see who the creep was who was saying such a personal thing to me. There was nobody there. Then I heard it again, this time, more insistent.

" HOLD ME !"

It slowly dawned on me that it was the tree talking to me.

I know, I know, this sounds absolutely ridiculous, doesn't it? It would be logical to accuse me right now of being mentally ill, or intoxicated or both. If only it were that simple to explain away. I was, however, in a grief state so I was more sensitive than usual, inhabiting that strange liminal space in-between the world of the living and the dead.

I reached out my hand and placed it on a yoni-shaped scar where a large branch had been ripped off the main trunk.

Ouch.

Just writing that and I'm made aware of how symbolic that is to a mother who has just had her eldest daughter ripped away from her own family tree.

As soon as my palm connected with the gnarly wooden scar, a jolt of electricity shot up my arm and flooded my heart space.

"Thank you! Thank you!" It vibrated back to me.

Later, bewildered as to what had just happened, I turned to the Answer-to-everything machine that we call Google.

What does it mean when an Elder tree talks to you?

One of my more unusual Google searches to be sure. The answers that popped up were very intriguing.

The Elder tree was colloquially known as the Gypsy tree, one must treat her with respect. Removing branches without first asking permission could result in the thief being cursed. It was also mentioned that the Elder served as a portal for communication with all other trees, so I presumed I'd been duly initiated into the subtle art of tree whispering.

I thought back to my recent obsession with elderflower cordial, and wondered if by imbibing the tree's energetic essence, I had somehow allowed it access to communicate directly through me.

That's my theory, I told you I'd get around to it eventually.

What other strange and mysterious thing was to happen next?

My life seemed to be throwing up all sorts of adventures.

Who is Imogen?

I mogen is my firstborn daughter, born on New Year's Eve when the fireworks were exploding in the dark, midnight sky. Interestingly enough, she too was like a firework: intense, explosive, brilliant, awesome and sadly, short-lived. Born after a protracted 36 hour labour, with a lengthened distorted, moulded head and the cord wrapped tightly around her neck. It's not lost on me that exactly 28 years later, she would die with a different type of cord around her neck. Our firework burned herself out, bright and quickly, because if you try and extend a firework's life, you end up with a mere fizz.

Imogen was anything but a fizz. Her main battle was against her mind. One of her last conversations around this to me was when she had realised she was autistic. (She had been booked in for an urgent adult assessment that she just couldn't face). She had had the realisation that her brain was always going to be that way and for her this was simple untenable. She told me she didn't want her 'baby brain'. She'd rather have a brain that didn't cause her so much pain. Of course this was not possible.

Unfortunately she came to realise far too late that it was her capacity to feel pain that was part of her immense gift, her ability to feel so intensely that helped her create so much beauty and fuelled her creativity. When she secretly started using heroin in her final years to self-medicate, she realised this all too late. I later found drawings in her sketchbook where she;d depicted herself trying and failing, to touch stars, a poetic metaphor for her lost sparkle.

It was an icy, dark, depressing realisation that once she'd taken the pain away, she didn't know who she was.

She described her entire existence as like being on a roller-coaster that you could never get off, massive euphoric highs, followed by soul crushing zombie-like lows. Her nervous system was in constant fight, flight, fawn, freeze, flop mode which was an exhausting way to live one's life.

Initially diagnosed with and medicated for Rapid Cycling Bipolar disorder, (the DSM considers this more than four episodes of distinct mood episodes within a twelve month period) this still could not explain how she could go from ecstatic in the morning to suicidal in the evening.

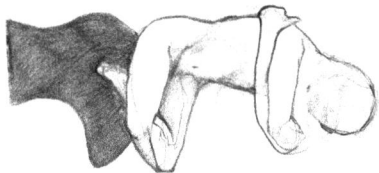

The frequency and intensity of her mood swings were far more dramatic than seemed to fit the pattern of this diagnosis. The medication she was given, seemed, if anything, to make her worse. She knew she wasn't 'normal' but how she felt on this medication took her even further away from herself. She had put all her faith in medication, looking for a magic silver bullet that would cure her and take all the pain away. The pain was her gift and her curse, this was the yin-yang paradox of being Imogen.

Imogen's highest highs were found through love, or put another way, obsession. This is now understood as autistic limerance, where hyper-fixation can bring massive highs but also because of the issue with interpreting social cues, is often an area of extreme challenge. This pattern of behaviour left her open to manipulation and abuse from romantic partners who didn't necessarily have her best interests at heart. Obsessional love made her come alive, but the intensity of giving and receiving this type of energy was ultimately unsustainable for her and her romantic focus.

Excerpt from Imogen's diary.
Saturday September 25 2010
My whole body buzzes when you are in my life.
Even if I don't see you, even if the enthusiasm that drives me on long walks, singing at the top of my voice goes utterly unreciprocated.

Even if I'm totally ignored.
Thank you for this feeling, thank you!

Like a roller-coaster, this obsession would reach a peak then completely drop away, leaving people people in her wake totally bewildered and flummoxed and Imogen would be left thinking she was an evil person for making people sad.

Excerpt from Imogen's diary.

The bull in my dreams just kept charging at me. It didn't care about anyone else, just had to hurt me, even kill me. I felt like saying,
"What have I done that makes you want to hurt me so badly?"
because I'm so afraid that I'm hurting people without even realising, that's how cold I am inside. I can't even recognise basic human emotion.

Whether the obsession was for Gormenghast, Vic and Bob, the Tigerlillies, The Mighty Boosh or jacket potatoes, (she had eclectic obsessions) they were all intensely focused upon.

When she grew into puberty, these were largely replaced by music and her latest romantic interest. This was usually the person nearest to her who gave her any attention.
Social cues were misunderstood and misinterpreted, this resulted in her falsely believing she lacked empathy. The opposite was actually true. Imogen would hyper-empathise to her significant (for that moment) other to such a degree that she absorbed them, she became them along with the resultant loss of identity that brought with it.

When the relationships ended, she understood she was hurting people and this pain caused her deep shame and remorse. She struggled to understand how to stop this cycle of obsession and abandonment. She didn't know how to love any other way. She was an all or nothing girl.

Once she met Rob, her future husband, her pattern seeking brain, intense journaling and self reflection, had helped her identify that this beautiful, yet dark, soul relationship, had an inbuilt expiry date. She wanted to hold on to him forever and to be able to cheat her brain and it's patterns. Heroin inevitably skewed her thinking during these times also, taking away any access to hope or positivity. I also believe that heroin severs the connection to the higher self, making it impossible to feel supported in any spiritual manner.

So tragically, she did what she did. It wasn't an impulsive decision, it was meticulously planned, and Rob agreed to follow her down this dark path. He wrote in her journal that it was his birthday gift to her and this was also echoed in many song lyrics. I've spoken to some of Rob's close family members who've reassured me that he too had his demons. With Imogen's tendency to absorb the identity and mood of her lovers, it was almost written in the stars that they'd follow each other down that dark path back home eventually.

Imogen's diary excerpt (one month before she died)

Taking baby steps away from worlds that gutted me and finding myself longing for the bits I tried hardest to leave. I want to be a purer me, a more whole me some day, but the brain-antagonist shouts louder every day. I want to be a world away and absolutely free from everything that's hounded me, from everything that's swallowed me. I want to be a concentrated form of myself where the parts that only held me down are thrown into the air. Can I still edge oblivionwhilst reaching for the moon? Can I still take the numbness and discard the foggy gloom?

We came here for a specific reason with very makeshift, half thought through plans to die and release ourselves from the endless cycle of pain that is being us, with an afterthought that an epiphany might stick things back together neatly and might give us the environment to thrive.

I wish there had been another way. I wish I could hear her throaty laugh and see her deep in bliss while she danced and sang playing her guitar, barefoot on the stage once more.

But surrender I must. This was her journey. I had to let her go.

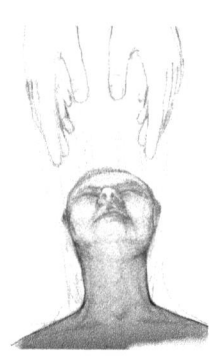

Part 2 Little Diane in Kansas

My Birth

In Spring, 1964, my mother, newly married, went into labour in hospital. Her baby was in a breech position. In the early 1960s, maternity care was expected to take place in the hospital as the birth experience became increasingly medicalised. Women in labour would be given castor oil enemas routinely, a bath and then would be expected to birth flat on their backs with legs in stirrups to allow the doctor a good view of the proceedings. It was not unheard of for midwives to slap 'hysterically' labouring women. Because of a chronic shortage of midwives at the time (nothing seems to have shifted there) many women gave birth alone. My mother must have been terrified and rightfully so. She had just turned 20 and her baby was coming out the wrong way.

Trust me to be difficult right from the start. All mum told me is that I was a forceps birth so I was pulled out with metal spoons, not the most pleasant of experiences for mum. She must have been traumatised.

Once I was delivered, a skinny baby of 6 lbs, (mum was a smoker during pregnancy) mum suffered the indignity of being told by a male doctor that because she had small breasts, she would end up starving her baby if she tried to breastfeed. What absolute misogynistic ignorance that was. I was promptly bottle fed from that moment onwards.

Nothing much was shared with me about my infant years except for two quite significant things.

The first was I used to 'head-bang' in order to soothe myself to sleep. Mum would put me on the sofa at bedtime and the family would watch me, bemusedly while I rocked and banged my tiny self against the back of the sofa until I fell asleep. I can still find comfort in this action as an adult to this day, and at times of dysregulation can soothe myself by banging my back against a wall.

The second quirk I demonstrated, was a strong dislike for food as a weaning toddler. Mum saw it that way, but I strongly believe it was not to do with taste as much as texture. This was my sensory sensitivities showing themselves from a young age. Mum told me that she would tie me to the high chair to stop me swatting the food away. It sounds really cruel but I can imagine mum's fear of her baby not eating. Still I feel sad for little me not having her preferences honoured at such a formative age. It is interesting for me to observe my preferences as an adult for squishy mouth feel foods. They bring me deep comfort.

4

Mum's early years

I had always been fascinated as a child by my mother's tiny breasts. They were barely an A cup but she had very well developed nipples, her breasts resembling cup cakes with cherries on the top. She had always been self-conscious of her breasts, as her mother had considerable breasts rather like my own. I've often speculated if my mother's impaired breast development was somehow linked to the sudden loss of her father when she was ten years old.

In 1954 her father, James, went off to his bricklaying job as normal and never returned home, having suffered a fatal cardiac arrest at work. He was in his late 30's, a thin, wiry man. No one could've predicted this sudden, tragic loss. The devastation this loss would wreak on my mother would pass down through the years and go on to impact her children and grandchildren. She never got over her father's death. Her mother was advised at the time, rightly or wrongly, to not allow her youngest children to attend the funeral in case it traumatised them. I believe this was a mistake as mum never had a chance to really understand and process her father's death as something real. She would speak of how she had always expected him to walk through the door one day. The death had created a huge abandonment wound in my mother that she would never manage to heal. Later on in my life I would go on to experience first hand, just how hard it is to grieve the loss of a parent without any chance of closure.

Mum piled on weight, the result of the combination of adolescence and the impact of cortisol from grief. She was horribly bullied about her body by staff and pupils alike at her brand new Grammar school. Mum recounted a story of a time she was doing PE in the school hall and her foot went through the floor. It was probably a structural defect or the result of an old decaying floorboard, but mum was relentlessly bullied for being too fat for the floor to hold her weight, by the teacher in front of the whole giggling class. I'm sure this was the trauma seed that started her lifelong bulimia problem. Another incident she recounted was the head teacher pulling her up in the dining hall, humiliating her once again by pointing out where she had spilled food down her top, saying " You dirty, dirty girl'.

I'm convinced mum was singled out for being poor as well as fat. This gives me insight into why she grew up hating on my fat body and not wanting me to go into a career where I struggled to earn good money. Still I wondered why mum still wanted me to attend the same school where she was so horrendously treated.

After my grandfather's sudden death, my nan had been left a single mother of four, and they were dirt poor, sharing shoes and making do, marching around the house banging on pots and pans for entertainment. My mother getting a place at the posh local Grammar school was a big deal but being the poor kid in among the other privileged children must have left her even more stigmatised and vulnerable. Grammar school was considered the only path out of poverty in her family's situation, meaning she must have felt she had to suck up all the abuse she received there. It was the price you had to pay. Mum being clever was her way out of what must've felt like a desperate environment.

Mum was born in 1944 in the middle of WWII, her mother's womb must've been a sea of cortisol. Her dad was away fighting and her mum had two other children to take care of alone. Mum was a middle child, with two older siblings, a brother and a sister and a younger brother, Stephen, whom she doted on. She would look after her little brother while her mum was out at one of her many jobs, trying her best to make ends meet. Mum and Uncle Stephen would often stay over at their maternal grandparents house .

Great-granddad was a hard man, some might say cruel. His wife had been left disabled from a bout of polio and she walked with the aid of a stick. One of the few family legends spoken about him was that he had at one point, beaten up his wife with her own walking aid and thrown her down the stairs in a fit of rage. The type of man subject to bouts of domestic violence of that degree I would not trust around children. Unfortunately, due to childcare needs, my mum as an 11 year old and her 6 year old baby brother would regularly stay over at this dangerous house. I can't help speculating that something must have happened to both my mum and my uncle during that time given their strange dynamic as siblings that would continue far into the future.

5

The Ballad of Uncle Stephen

It is 2004 and my mother has just emailed me from South Africa to ask me to do her a favour.

My childhood favourite uncle, Uncle Stephen, had been arrested and held in Lincoln prison on remand, on a charge of sexually assaulting his eldest daughter. My mother vehemently denied any possibility of this being true and rushed to her baby brother's defence. She asserted it was all a big misunderstanding and that this was obviously the result of the bitter ex-wife creating a vendetta against him, grooming her daughter to make false allegations against her father. My mother wanted to send letters of support to her brother whilst he was on remand to keep his spirits up, and she'd worked out the quickest way to get them to him was if she sent me emails. Since she was in South Africa at the time, this made sense. I agreed that I'd print them out for her and post them off from London, but I had no intention of supporting my uncle because by this point I knew him categorically to be a paedophile. The news of the charge of sexual assault of his daughter, whilst shocking, did not come as a surprise.

A few months prior to this news, I had had an illuminating conversation with my younger female cousin. Uncle Stephen's sister's child.

She was a few years younger than I. When catching up after returning from my time out in South Africa, I told her about the time Uncle Steve would take me out on 100 mph secret drives on the motorway just before we emigrated. After listening, she went quiet for a while, then with tears in her eyes, she sighed heavily and said.

"After you left, he took me driving on the motorway too. We also had chips and curry sauce and I was told it was our secret. Then after about a month, he raped me."

Stunned silence.

I responded, quietly and intensely,
"I'm so sorry love, you didn't deserve that. I will never forgive him for the harm he did to you and possibly others too."

Right at that point I realised just what a lucky escape I'd had, literally in the nick of time. It was like mum knew or something... I thought back to what mum had said when she was around ten years old, after she had just lost her dad. She used to go and stay with her granddad, the one who beat up his disabled wife, and she was responsible for looking after her little brother, who would've been around six years old. Uncle Stephen had grown up to be a paedophile. My mum was incapable of talking to me about sex or rape, but also had denied my own reality around such things. Was she holding on to her own dark secrets and trying to make up for her guilt around not being able to protect her baby brother? Her being in such strong denial around the possibility of her brother being a sexual predator hinted at the possibility of this being true.

I read the first printed out e-mail that mum wanted me to send on to Uncle Stephen. In it she told him that everyone in the family was supporting him and that they all knew he was innocent and he'd be out of jail soon, as clearly these were trumped up charges. She even had the audacity of name checking me, saying I personally sent my love and support. That was going to far, not in my name. I emailed mum back, furiously telling her that there was no possibility of my sending that letter to him unless she edited out every mention of my name. Mum was bamboozled. Why wasn't I supporting him?

I responded, " Because , Mum, he's a predator. I believe his daughter and I have good reason to know that she is telling the painful truth."

Uncle Stephen pleaded guilty at Lincoln Crown Court and was sent to Lincoln prison to do a stretch at Her Majesty's pleasure. He said he'd pleaded guilty to all charges to avoid having his daughter take the witness stand and testifying. He said he'd rather not traumatise her.

Either he was showing compassion and accountability or he feared what his daughter might say if she took the stand, I'm not sure which one it was.

A few months later, Uncle Stephen found himself on an aeroplane, bound for South Africa, Middle-of -Nowhere's- Ville, (VanWyksdorp) to stay (or hide out?) with his big sister. I have no idea if he avoided jail time or skipped the country when on probation, but it was clearly time for his big sister to protect him once more.

My mother would go on to write long emails to me about her idyllic time out in the South African countryside with her baby brother. I pondered over their strange, inconsistent relationship. There was a time twenty years earlier, when my Uncle had gone missing for a good ten years after absconding with the Fire Station Charity collection funds. My mum had had no communication with him then at all and seemed not the slightest bit worried or concerned about his whereabouts . Her mother, my Nan, was beside herself with worry, frantically looking for her lost adult youngest child. He was eventually tracked down with the help of the Salvation Army through his car registration number. He was was running a bar and living it up in the sunshine on the Costa Del Crime, somewhere in Spain and was not exactly delighted to have been found. He was promptly arrested and did his first stint in prison. At least this time my Nan knew where he was. My mum didn't talk to me about this at all, in fact I only found out by speaking to my Nan as an adult.

So I found it very odd that my mum was suddenly best friends with her baby brother .

It wasn't to last.

Six months later, mum emailed me to tell me she'd had a massive fight with Steve over cigarettes (yes, that sounds like typical mum drama) and she'd chucked him out to fend for himself.

Uncle Stephen, ever resourceful, went to live on a neighbouring farm owned by a couple he'd befriended who had an eleven year old daughter...

He died of cancer a year later.

6

It's Normal to Kiss Strangers

Little Diane loved her mumy with a passion even though mummy could be scary at times. She was pretty and clever at making long frilly dresses in bold patterned fabric on her treadle Singer sewing machine. I would wear these dresses to my school discos with pride, no-one ever had a dress like mine.

Mum and Dad on their wedding day

My Daddy was also so handsome. People would say he looked like James Dean and. he was a star in the local football team. He was funny, silly and kind but he would give me the sloppiest of kisses when his breath smelled like booze. I didn't like that at all and would wipe away the slobber unceremoniously as Dad laughed at my clear disgust.

Back in the 70's, kids were expected to kiss strange adults who were there at bedtime (in my case, friends of my parents round for a game of cards) on the lips. I hated it, but I was a good girl who did as she was told so I dutifully puckered up and with each kiss, repeated the night time mantra:
"Good night, I love you, God bless."
Afterwards they always chuckled which I found very confusing. What was so funny? Were they mocking me?

Bedtime for me was 6.30pm and my bedroom was upstairs. We had just got a brand new colour telly and Top of the Pops was my favourite program. However, that started at 7pm, so I would sneak downstairs and sit on the bottom stair and watch the exciting music show through the crack in the door.

Every so often I'd sit there too when mum and dad were having one of their many loud, screaming fights in the kitchen. I'd sit on the stair and sob and ask my fairy friends to make them stop.

7

My Relationship with Fairies

Fairies were my earliest friends. I would watch them dance around my bedroom when the sun shone through my buttercup yellow curtains, bright specks of light that darted from place to place.

I had a massive picture book, it was as big as I was, so big it had to be kept in the airing cupboard on the landing as it couldn't fit on any bookshelf. Inside were ethereal watercolour paintings of fairies in a fairy glen. If it had text, I hadn't noticed, I was so transfixed with wonder at the visual magic inside that giant cardboard cover. I would spend hours pouring over those pages, escaping to a fantasy place of magical possibility. I had decided from an early age that I wanted to be a fairy when I grew up.

Looking back at this memory as a 60 year old, I cannot quite separate the knowing of the reality of those fairies from the book. It was like the fairies were contained in a separate universe inside the pages of the book that would manifest once I opened up that enormous cardboard cover. A portal to another universe perhaps, where things were less shouty and more predictable.

8

A Scruffy Fairy Alter Ego and a Symbolic Tattoo

Fairies continued to be in my life as I grew into adulthood. In my role as a children's entertainer, I would create a large arm puppet that would teach me about my unmasked self. Her name was Fifi the Baby Fairy. I created this chaotic fairy baby puppet because I had a vague idea that I wanted to be able to speak through a character that had permission to always tell the truth about what she saw with no filter.

    I had always been fascinated by babies that I saw on the bus, witnessing how they would stare deep into stranger's souls, unflinchingly, as if trying to unlock this strangers' deepest secrets. This held enormous comedic potential for me and comedy was at the root of my act. Silly paid my bills. It was a serious business being a professional silly person. Silly had the capacity to enchant an entire room of tiny strangers and hold them in my thrall, like magic. If I could make the little ones laugh, I knew the party would be a success. I had to walk into a room of strange little children and make an instant bond with them. This was the way.

Having an open heart and a silly soul sprinkled with a little (well, a lot) of subversive (mischievous) humour, seemed to be my secret formula for instantly bonding with children under 6 years old. In the 25 years of my puppeteering life, I'd never met a child I couldn't win over.

Adults, however were another matter entirely.

Like in all my creative endeavours, whether it was creating wearable art robes, painting on canvas or entertaining groups of young children with puppets, I worked in a flow state. Everything I did was improvised, done in the moment, then built upon in real time. As soon as I pulled out this tanned-skinned, iridescent-eyed, feathered-headed, wobbly-wanded creature, she seemed to spring to a life of her own. I would often tell people with genuine bewilderment that this puppet had the ability to tell me jokes where I had no idea of the punchline. It was if this character was accessing a deep, possibly dissociated part of myself to animate this bundle of sparkly rags and feathers into this charismatic, mischievous, unpredictable character who could charm boys and girls alike and intimidate the adults who pretended to have authority over her. I met many a male headteacher who deeply feared this fairy puppet. I now understand that Fifi was the embodiment of the part of me called Pathological Demand Avoidance. Well, that's what the men in suits call it. Those of us that live with this quirk prefer to call it Pervasive Drive for Autonomy.

My darling, challenging, unfiltered granddaughter would go on to teach me all about this aspect of myself, as her behaviour at first seemed like defiance, but then we understood as deep anxiety and 'stuckness' once a demand was placed on her.

I would personally encounter this same feeling in a dance workshop, as my body spun me out of a formation of a 'Simon Says' type of exercise, physically throwing me into the corner of the room in a fit of anxiety after what I perceived as a massive demand. All I had been asked to do was follow a leader and do a physical action. Not so hard, you may think. Well clearly, for me it was. My brain prevented me from doing this in a very melodramatic manner. I ended up a sobbing mess in the corner of the room, dancing in my own way, telling myself I could do it the way I wanted to do it.

This was a very clear demonstration of my PDA core which had been deeply masked for years. Now I know I had created Fifi the Baby Fairy as a way of channelling it into something useful. Once of the key characteristics of this part of autism is that PDA kids and adults do not automatically respond to authority. We do not see hierarchy. We are very logical creatures and respect has to be earned. Justice is paramount and rules are only followed if they are fair and make logical sense. Rules are then rigidly adhered to and we get anxious if we witness others transgressing them. If the rules don't make logical sense, however, we feel completely justified to ignore them. Fifi was the complete embodiment of this quirk of my personality (or you could argue, aspect of my neurodivergence.)

During the time of my being a children's entertainer, I hadn't any clue of my own neurodivergence. I thought that everyone was like me. Now I can see that my ability to spontaneously create routines with my puppet, was a skill that belonged to my deeply connected, pattern-seeking brain that thrived on risk and being in the moment to be able to show itself to it's best ability.

One of Fifi's most memorable moments was when I was asked to be part of a voluntary art project working inside the locked ward at Springfield Mental hospital. A visiting therapist reached out to me in my capacity as a puppeteer, and asked me if I'd like to work alongside her on a puppet-making workshop. I jumped at this unusual opportunity even though there was no money involved. The practical side of the puppet-making was challenging as I was given a long list of proscribed items that would be a risk factor in this secure unit. After a bit of out-of-box thinking, I came up with the idea of pre-making basic foam shapes that could be fastened together with double-sided tape, along with various 'wigs' made from pre-cut lengths of yarn and sticky-backed tape for easy self assembly. Along with a bag of socks and various bits of fabric for the puppet body, this created a viable and effective solution. The hours of preparation were worth it when I saw the people in the unit responding so positively to this activity. The experience for me was heartbreaking, though, For the duration of the week of that project, I would return home and cry every day as the illusion of them and us completely dissolved and disintegrated as I realised that every human being was only one breakdown away from losing all freedom and sense of self.

As part of this project, I took Fifi along as she had always helped me feel more confident in myself in new surroundings and social settings. I could use Fifi to redirect attention away from me and towards my puppet. Performing my fairy was much easier than performing being Diane the human.

On the first day of entering the secure unit, I was introduced by the visiting therapist to the resident psychiatrist, a young man who had recently joined the unit. The therapist hinted that he was considered a bit of a genius boy wonder. He was fascinated with Fifi and chatted with her directly, eagerly. Then he took me around the unit, introducing me to the other members of staff by saying, "Do the fairy thing." I politely obliged, not quite knowing how to refuse, but something felt off.

Afterwards I was asked to help encourage some of the more reticent people in the unit to come and join the workshop. A small proportion of them were very vulnerable, clearly deep in a state of psychosis or altered reality, but somehow Fifi managed to penetrate their world with her mischievous open heart and these people then engaged in the activity to the best of their abilities. What was most notable was that Fifi had brought laughter to a place that was jigsaws with missing pieces, cigarette smoke and constant Jeremy Kyle show on the televisions on the walls. Surely that had to be a positive thing?

A week after the project ended, I received an e-mail from the therapist who's project it had been. She thanked me for my participation at the unit but said that no plans were in place for any future such projects. This was because during the ward rounds afterward, the new 'boy wonder' psychiatrist had made a throwaway remark in his excitement for the project to the consultants who were touring the ward with him. He spoke of a puppeteer who had been around the more vulnerable people in the ward with a fairy. The senior members of the team did not like the idea of some "tree-hugger, do-gooder, arty-farty type" supporting and entering the delusions of the sectioned people in the ward. So they had forbidden any further such projects.

No more laughter in the ward. Back to Jeremy Kyle, chain smoking and missing puzzle pieces then.

During the time of my life when I could have easily found myself sectioned and in a locked ward myself, I would go on to get my only tattoo, a very rigid, gothic fairy, sitting on a cloud holding up a wand, over my heart.

Normally when people get tattoos they spend hours contemplating the image and planning the symbolism and placement of this permanent marking on their body. Not me. The day I found myself getting this black haired, badly drawn fairy tattooed on my breast, I had not even intended having a tattoo at all.

I had found myself at a shoddy tattoo place in the heart of Brixton market (it no longer exists, thankfully) because I had agreed to pay for a very expensive tattoo for the friend of my abusive partner at the time. Coercive control comes in many forms, of which this one clearly one. As I stood at the desk, paying for this virtual stranger's tattoo, I impulsively decided to get one of my own. The very first fairy I saw in their sample book was the one I decided upon in my haste and chaotic mindset.

She has turned out to be the perfect reminder of my clay feet and my vulnerability.

She is the only tattoo I have and the only one I've ever needed.

9

The Grecian Dress and Infidelity

Little Diane remembers her mummy being so pretty. One particular memory stands out of mummy looking just like a princess. Her hair was styled up in a coiffed, elegant beehive with sparkling jewelled clips in it, and she was wearing a flowing Grecian style draped white dress with silver sparkles and silver strappy shoes to match. She looked breathtaking to my 5-year-old eyes.

I woke up later that evening to loud shouting again.

Mummy was crying. I peeped into my parents bedroom to see my dad ripping up the white dress as my mummy sobbed. On the surface, dad looks like the villain of this story. I'd come to learn, years later, that Mum had real problems with being faithful in her marriage(s). That fateful night, she'd entered (and won) a local beauty pageant wearing that dress. She really did look so beautiful in it. My Dad had had reports from people attending the pageant that Mum was observed behaving very inappropriately with many of the men there (many of whom were Dad's mates from his football team.) So in a fit of jealousy, anger, humiliation and insecurity, my Dad had taken it all out on the dress.

Our neighbours on our Midlands council estate, a middle-aged very average looking couple with two young boys, were our friends. The two boys, who were around my age, would often knock for me to play. Many years later, I found out that when I was downstairs playing with my toys with the two brothers, their Daddy was playing different kinds of games with my Mummy upstairs while Dad was at work.

This pattern would continue to play out throughout Mum's life. Mum would continue to have affairs with multiple men, none of them particularly attractive or rich (not that that excuses anything) despite being very outwardly prudish. She would harshly criticise any woman who had children out of wedlock and thought that being married was the only respectable goal for a woman.

I wonder if her Romany ancestry had some influence over this?
Mum needed the validation of male gaze, like you and I need air to breathe.

10

Mum, Me and the Roses

Despite Mum's clear flaws she had many positive attributes, one that sticks out in my memory was her green fingers.

Mum was an excellent gardener and her passion was for roses, which she grew in abundance in our clay-rich front garden. There were the dainty and heady scented old-fashioned pink bush roses with their simple frilly single round of petals.

There were the deep, blood-red roses, dramatic and dark, almost black. The bright red roses that looked freshly painted by the playing card subjects of the Queen of Hearts. The pure white roses that had me pretending to be the playing card workers, playing out my Alice in Wonderland fantasies with my toy paintbrush and a bucket of imaginary red paint. The sweet smelling bright yellow roses and even a lilac rose that didn't look at all real. But the most beautiful rose of all in the garden was the Peace rose, a new hybrid at the time. It was a variegated peach and yellow beast of a bloom, with a deep perfume. I would bury my whole face in the rose, breathing in it's sweet scent and relishing the feel of the velvet petals against my child cheeks. As an only child for most of my youth, I spent many hours in the garden making potions from the rose petals, pretending to be a sorceress, a good witch of course. Being outside in nature but also inside my imagination was deeply soothing and fulfilling for me.

I couldn't understand why mum would cut back the roses so hard at the end of the blooming season. I remember watching her and feeling pain at witnessing my beloved roses reduced to what seemed like a stump. It seemed so cruel to me but they would grow back even stronger the following year.

What an interesting metaphor for Mum's parenting style, this was.

11

Make Believe Play

When I couldn't be outside, my indoors play was also very solitary and imaginative.

To the onlooker, it may have looked like I was just lining up my toys and organising my books, inside my head I would be reenacting many real-life scenarios including *Library Library, School School,* or *Shop Shop.*

The most fun was had by meticulously recreating the outside world inside my bedroom and rehearsing it, using appropriate scripts. I would make library date stamps from rubbers and stick borrowing cards inside my books after alphabetically arranging them and grading them for size and colour.

Shop Shop involved making price labels, then rearranging my stuff on make-believe shelves and pretending a drawer and box was a till. A pile of copper coins was a valued toy in my world.

Even on my visits to Nan's house, my favourite thing was sorting through her old, beautiful, battered button tin with a painting of a lady in a crinoline dress on the lid. I'd dip my hands and nose into the weighty sea of textures, metal, bone, shell and plastic, a sensory treat for my hands, nose and eyes.

Then of course, I'd spend hours sorting them all into piles before tipping them all back in to the tin for next time.

At school I was often the 'treasurer monitor' in charge of any money coming in for school trips or various activities. I took so much pride in sorting and counting money accurately.

To me it was just a fun game.

12

Early music influences

My red suitcase portable record player was always in use in my bedroom.

I would play my mum's extensive Motown record collection and Uncle Stephen's Reggae and Ska singles. I'd memorise every lyric, dance and sing along loudly if I thought no-one was around to hear me.

Aretha Franklin, Smokey Robinson and the Miracles, Al Green, Otis Redding, Harry J Allstars The Liquidator, Prince Buster's Al Capone, the soundtrack to the Aristocats, The Sound of Music and The Move were sounds of my early childhood.

My mum bought me a subscription to Jackie magazine that was delivered every Thursday. Donny Osmond peered down on me from the Jackie posters stuck all over my bedroom walls, covering up my babyish wallpaper, a sharp contrast to the musicians I actually preferred. I'm not sure my mum would have been comfortable with my having posters of the Jackson 5 instead. Jackie magazine seemed quite biased in their offering of candidates for the centrefold. For years mum would try to tease me about my apparent crush on Little Jimmy Osmond. This bewildered me as I didn't like him one bit. To be fair I didn't like his big brother Donny much either but he was the best of a bad bunch and did a decent job of covering up the cartoon wallpaper.

Mum and I did share a love for David Essex though. Cor, he was dishy.

Once I started getting pocket money, I was able to save up to by my first records. It felt so grown up to be able to make my own choices and not have to rely on mum's records (although to be fair she had great taste). I bought two albums, Gary Glitter's Do You Wanna Touch? and the Peer Gynt Suite by Grieg, because I loved In the Hall of the Mountain King with it's chaotic speeded-up ending. We did music and movement to that at school and it ignited my soul and I loved it with every fibre of my dancing body.

Earth, Wind and Fire on Top of the Pops would seep into my psyche with their Egyptian styling and syncopated grooves and would pop out of me in the form of wearable art later on in my life.

I would lose my taste for Gary Glitter quite quickly, something about him was weird.

The music was still good though.

13

Pets, Nature and Wales

One of the things I remain deeply grateful to my parents for, is the opportunity to have grown up around so many animals.

We had so many, you could have named it our menagerie. Dogs (my favourite), cats, birds (including briefly a rescued wild Jackdaw named Jack) guinea-pigs, fish, rabbits, hamsters (that insisted on repeatedly escaping into the cavity wall spaces in our home) and gerbils galore.

I'll never forget the trauma of mum telling me she'd flushed the baby gerbils down the toilet as they'd had too many babies and the adults were eating them. Nature can be so cruel sometimes.

Then there were the holidays. Every year, twice a year, we would wake up in the early hours of the dark morning. Mum and dad would pack the car (a purple Ford Estate with a thick white racing stripe down the middle) with pillows, blankets and clothes then squish me into the back seat on top of them before setting off on a nauseating long car journey to Wales from the Midlands. Those 4 hours in the back of the car seemed like the longest time. I struggled badly with motion sickness as a child (and still do to this day) and my dad would have to regularly pull the car over to the side of the road so I could vomit. No wonder I'm not a fan of travel. The Welsh adventures were epic though. We alternated between the coastal South and the mountainous North, explored castles, mines and quarries, (where dad and I, equipped with small hammers, would search for fossils and crystals). We clambered up dry waterfalls, wild-camped in forests, bathing in the river and drinking spring water complete with tiny freshwater shrimp. Entertainment at night once was a card game in our tent with a ripe-smelling shepherd who spoke no English.

The best place for me as a child was a place called Bosherston in Pembrokeshire. My dad was an avid fisherman and this place, with it's system of interconnected lily-pad lakes was fishing heaven. We'd start off with a cream tea at the quaint tea shop near the car park, then bellies full of jammy scones and clotted cream, we'd head off to the lily ponds with dad's fishing tackle through the green lush vegetation of the woodland path. I'd often go off on my own solitary adventures, on a treasure hunt through the woods searching for wild strawberry treasure, or I'd spend time belly down on the earth, immersed in grasses, delighting in their varied quivering seed heads and potential for weaving adventures. At the end of the long pathway past the ponds through the woodland, was the most beautiful unspoiled beach with rocky caves full of sea creatures and a sandy expanse of shell hunting potential. I'd indulge in my love for sand sculpture which I took way beyond simple sand castles. Mermaids were a favourite thing to build. I'd have permission to sculpt boobies and cover them with shells and seaweed hair. For a preteen girl this was my happy place. As I write this I'm made aware that my mum was often conspicuously absent in many of these memories. I have no idea where she was at the time, but I felt so safe and content, I really didn't care. When I was hungry, I'd simply follow the path back to dad who would be still sitting trying to catch the elusive pike in the lake.

These are all memories I treasure, sweet nuggets of concentrated, crystallised happiness that I would revisit in times of feeling animosity towards my parents (well, my mother) in later life. For the most part, my early years were happy ones. I was a biddable child, clever, extremely shy, serious, quiet, introspective, and had always preferred adult company so I seemed older than my years.

I also had some artistic talent that was starting to show up. In North Wales, in the slate quarries, I would pick up pieces of loose slate and discovered that you could easily scratch on to them and create drawings. I spent most of that holiday drawing wild animals onto bits of flat rock. A few years earlier I had drawn a different animal onto an inappropriate surface .

14

Drawing Dougal

It was 1970, I was 6 years old.

The Magic Roundabout, a psychedelic cartoon was popular on the television. It was the last thing I was allowed to watch before bedtime, so it was important to me. My mum had just wallpapered my bedroom with brand new, expensive Magic Roundabout themed wallpaper. It had to have been a labour of love. I can imagine how difficult it must have been and how much care she would have had to put in to match up the various characters printed onto the pristine white paper. She proudly showed me her handiwork and I cooed in childish approval. Then mum went downstairs and I remained upstairs in my freshly decorated bedroom with a box of brand new wax crayons that I was itching to use. I didn't have any drawing paper, but my eyes caught the big white spaces on the wall in between the printed Magic Roundabout characters and I proceeded to copy Dougal the dog, with a big, fat yellow crayon into the empty space next to it. I stood back and admired my handiwork and remembered feeling extremely proud of the accuracy of my drawing.

I called mum upstairs to come and see what I had done.

Mum screamed, picked up my hairbrush and started chasing round the house threatening to paddle my bottom with the implement. This was not the reaction I was expecting. I ran away but alas, she was much faster than I and I had no chance at all. I did notice that by the time she caught me she was laughing but still proceeded to hit me. I had no idea what I had done wrong and I was totally flummoxed. My mother was perplexing to me, why was she hitting me and laughing? That felt really sinister. Hadn't I done a good drawing?

15

Nan through my eyes

Mummy and I are going to stay with Nan for a bit, yey! I wonder why Daddy isn't coming with us?

I love my Nan's house, it's cosy and it smells nice. It is a bit messy (not like our house) but it feels like a warm hug. Nan always brings out my favourite button tin. I like sitting in Nan's squishy big chair in front of her open fire to sort through it, surrounded by her assorted ornaments, wooden carved African animals, brasses and purple crystals called amethyst.

Afterwards, I hope she makes me my favourite cheese, tomato, and potato bake which I'll gobble up with a dash of ketchup and a dollop of chutney. After that I'll go upstairs to bed and cuddle up next to her in her lumpy but wonderful feather bed and my sleepy eyes will trace the pattern of the faded pink roses on the wallpaper before falling asleep. Even her outdoor toilet is an adventure.

Nan just feels safe. She has big, squishy breasts that I call her pillows and she lets me sleep on them if I'm upset. She strokes my hair and sings daft songs that they used to sing during the war.

I love my Nan.

Except for the time when I asked her if the Ancient Britons were alive when she was a little girl. She got angry with me then and that felt scary. Oh yes, and that time I pointed out to her with curiosity that she had a moustache.

She looked sad when I said that.

I don't know why.

I was just telling the truth like mummy tells me to.

16

Early Education

Before the age of ten, I had managed to attend three schools. The first school was at two years old. It was a nursery that I remembered being out in the woods. Mum would drive me there bright and early in the mornings before she left for work. I absolutely loved it there. There was a resident goat plus the opportunity to explore the small woodland area attached to the nursery at play time. However, even at such a tender age, there was a bully. His name was Nicky (he must've been around three years old at the time) and true to his name, he would nick my lunchtime sandwiches from me. I didn't mind handing over the dripping (beef lard) sandwiches because those were yucky, but I really didn't like it when he stole my jam ones.

My biggest memory from that time was the joy I felt cleaning up the watercolour paint pans, fastidiously rinsing off the mud-colour mixed-up paint and restoring the jewel-like colours to their pristine best, in their white ceramic containers. It's interesting that I remember this more fondly than I did doing actual paintings.

My second school was closer to my Nan's home and was a traditional primary school. I have very few memories of this time, maybe I was enrolled there when Mum had separated from Dad for a while, I can only speculate.

One memory that sticks out was winning the sack race on Sports Day. I had inadvertently cheated. Mum had provided me with a slippery pillow case to substitute for the usual rough hessian sack. Lack of friction for the win!

The other memory was playing with my good friend, the wind, at break times.

While the other children were running around screaming playing KissChase (my idea of hell), my six-year-old self was having the best time on my own, arms outstretched running down the slope towards the fence at the back of the school grounds, with the wind behind me. For all intents and purposes, I was flying.

I would get lost in this reverie, it would just be me and the wind, together in flight.

I'm still inclined to this day, as a woman now over 60 to stretch out the arms of my kimono and remember flying whenever the wind picks up. It feels so good as I connect with the elements and my playful inner child. I care not for the curious stares of the passers by in the park. I now own the coveted role of the local eccentric woman. It is an honour to be her.

My third and favourite school was a few hundred yards away from Mum and Dad's house.

It was a brand new school, an exciting new experiment in education. It was very close in concept to the radical Free School experiment that began in London in the 60s. There was no obvious hierarchy, teachers and parents worked in tandem, we called the teachers by their first names and there was no uniform. Classrooms were all open plan, except for curtained off 'quiet spaces', and there were no fixed lessons or age separated classes. Each pupil was individually assessed on their educational needs and potential and had a series of tailored work-cards drafted. The progress of these tasks was plotted on charts made available on display in the quiet areas which was quietly motivating.

Once these tasks were completed and assessed, the pupil was free to partake in their choice of activities that were freely available, ranging from sports and games including chess, all types of arts and crafts, from painting to perspective drawing and woodwork, pottery and enamelling. Drama and music, working on the school play, needlework or helping another pupil with their studies (peer learning). The choices were wide ranging and non-gendered. I realised I benefited wildly from this experiment as it was a perfect fit for my learning style. I flew ahead as I was a precocious reader and finished my work cards as quickly as possible to get to dive into the 'good stuff.'

Without my having had this school learning environment, I doubt whether my capacity to tackle various creative projects without fear would have developed as strongly.

I'm not sure how long this school remained this way, as research has shown that it was shut down many years ago. I doubt the political will would have remained to support this very progressive style of education. It would probably be described as 'woke' nowadays. I wish we had the courage as a nation to trust the innate creative potential of our people and give those who think outside the box opportunities to be educated in a similar manner to this school.

Now I realise just how fortunate I was to have had this start in life. It also explains why my Neurodivergence did not cause me any issues at school because this school environment perfectly suited the Neurodivergent neurotype. It also explains why my Neurodivergence remained masked for so long, as the early educational environment did not cause me distress, like schools do today. It is a shame that we can only recognise Neurodivergence through distress. Once we are distressed, we are called 'disordered' due to the fact that we are struggling to function in an environment that does not suit our needs. Adapt the environment to suit everyone, then no-one is disordered. This school proved this beautifully.

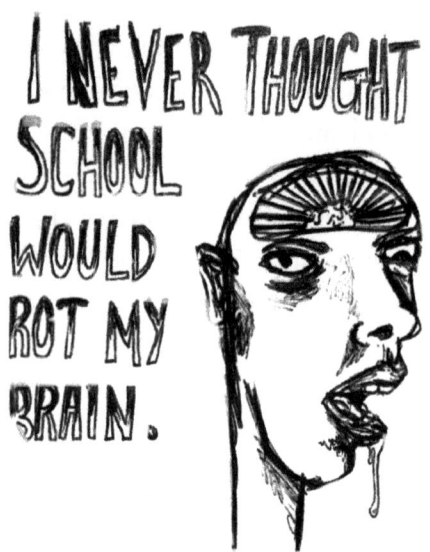

Image found in one Imogen's many journals during her time at secondary school

Currently our neurodivergent children are forced to mask to fit into the constraints of the rigid mainstream school system, causing massive dysregulation once they return home. This is not sustainable to the children's nervous systems (or the mental health of the struggling parents dealing with a dysregulated child) and leads to inevitable EBSA (emotionally based school avoidance).

For those parents who manage, against all odds, to get their neurodivergent children to attend mainstream school, they risk facing systemic parent blame for the behaviour of their dsyregulated children who are dysregulated as a result of having to endure the mainstream school environment.

It is a national scandal that is yet to be named. I pray for massive change in the school system so that our neurodivergent community can thrive instead of being punished by the neurotypical system. Shockingly, parents of neurodivergent children are currently being fined through the court system for not being able to get their children into school. Some parents are facing jail time. Often there is a child at home who is burnout and possibly suicidal, not able to attend school because the environment is not conducive to their needs. Why do we punish the parents who are desperately crying out for help for their child? What more are we expected to do?

On a personal level, educationally I had been blessed experiencing the experimental school as a pre-teen. Socially, maybe not so much.

During my time there, I had two best friends.

Or so I thought.

17

Clifford and the Valentine's card

There is a boy I like in my school called Clifford. He has long hair and a pretty face and is quite a bit shorter than me (well everyone my age is, to be fair) .He gives me those tummy wiggles and makes my cheeks red and hot when he looks at me.

I invited him back to my house for lunch during school lunch break. (I am allowed to go home for lunch seeing that it is so close by). I have a key to our house around my neck that I use to let myself in, It made me feel so grown-up. (I'm nine, but soon I'll be ten!) I made him beans on toast. We ate in silence then it got really awkward and I started to panic. I had no words or ideas of what to say so I did the first thing my panicking brain told me to do. I got up, stood over him in a bossy way and ordered him to do the washing up! It felt good standing behind him watching him wash up. It felt... sexy? Is this what sexy is?

All I knew is that things didn't feel awkward anymore. It worked, I think?

The next Valentine's Day (the most important day in the whole year, except for Christmas) I got a card from a secret admirer. The writing inside was all wobbly like when people use their wrong hand to write with, like Santa's letters to me used to look. I knew who it was from. It was so obvious.

I took it to school and proudly waved it about. The other kids giggled and cheered. I knew it was from Clifford. I stared at him and looked at the card. He shook his head and turned the other way, avoiding my stare. I figured I'd embarrassed him in front of the other kids and he was just trying to play it cool. I'd heard boys did that. It was just a boy thing.

When I got home my Nan was there. She asked me if I liked her Valentines card that she'd sent me.

I pulled out 'Clifford's ' card.

" This one?" I asked hesitantly.
"Yes!" she responded, " I love you, DeeDee Dinah!"
I didn't feel the same way towards my Nan in that moment.

Why do people lie?

18

First Boys Party

It's my big birthday coming up and I'm so excited! I'm turning double digits, ten! Mum says I can have a proper birthday party at home and I can invite boys! (What has got into her? She's never let me have boys at a party before.)

Mum seems very excited, almost more excited than me, which is weird. It's not her birthday. She's made me a birthday dress, although I'd prefer to wear my flared jeans that are covered with butterfly patches. Obviously I'll wear the dress, I wouldn't want to disappoint Mum. It's pretty, long, with a deep frill on the hem. It's made in a flowery pattern in the colours of our bathroom, lilac and red, with a dash of pink. I'm surprised it isn't purple, like our living room, car and Dad's best suit. My parents really seem to like purple.

Mum has bought a red light bulb for my bedroom. I didn't even know you could make light red, but I love it. It makes me feel all glowy and calm. She seems a bit amused by the red light, is there something I'm missing?

Mum's been cooking. She's made my favourite cheese pastry swirls, mini sausage rolls and loads of sandwiches with the crusts cut off. I made little flags with cocktail sticks and paper to say what's inside the sandwiches. I also helped her make the cheese and pineapple foil potato hedgehog. No party is complete without one of those! Everything looks so good.

I feel a bit worried just in case too many people show up.
I spent ages making the invitations , all twenty of them for my whole class and I handed them all out.
Obviously I invited Clifford, my best friends Dawn and Tracey and Tracey's brother, David. If they all come, my bedroom will be a bit squished and the thought of that makes me feel funny. Anyhow I better not think about that too much.
I've sorted out all my best records to play and have blown up so many balloons, my head is spinning.

Okay I'm ready.

I sit watching the clock as it ticks slowly and loudly.
Tick, tick, tick.

I shout downstairs,
"Mum, has anyone knocked yet?"
"Not yet..." she answers.

I wait until bedtime. Pop the silly balloons and turn off the silly red light. I take off my party dress and leave it in a heap on the floor. I don't even feel like eating the cheese swirls. I hug my teddy as I climb underneath my yellow candlewick bedspread and fiddle with the tufts, angrily pulling out quite a few. Then I pull the yellow cover over my head and cry myself to sleep.

I'm so embarrassed.
No-one came.

I never want to have a party ever again.

19

Social Struggles and my First Period

Dawn and Tracey are ganging up on me again. I don't understand what I did wrong?

Usually they are nice to me but now they are sniggering behind my back. That doesn't feel nice but I still want to be their friend. I wonder if they are talking about not coming to my party? Are they laughing at me or am I just being paranoid? Tracey's brother, David is always really nice to me and it somehow feels easier to be his friend, but I can't be his friend without being Tracey's friend. It's all so complicated and annoying.

When Dawn and Tracey are nice to me, we have lots of fun together and we chat about the boys on the estate. We even made up a song about them.

We love you Richard, we love you true,
We love you Chris, and Johnny too.
We hope that you will love us too
With a love so sweet and new.

I was the milk-monitor at school, in charge of handing out the bottles of free milk at break-time. I always looked forward to this, both being in charge and drinking the milk.

One day I had a belly ache. I thought it was perhaps the milk.

When I got home I found blood in my knickers.

I had a feeling I knew what this was as mum had something a few months ago about me becoming a woman soon but I wasn't really listening because it was just too embarrassing. What was more annoying for me in this moment, though, was now I had to tell mum about this.

Ugh, that's awkward.

I waited until mum was in the bath, then I casually walked in and said,

" Mum, I've joined you."

She wasn't too sure what I meant, unsurprisingly.

Ugh, that's so annoying. Why don't you get it? I thought to myself, too scared to actually utter those words. Was she really going to make me say it?

"I've started my period!" I shouted perhaps a little too loudly, and stomped out of the bathroom, slamming the door.

Later I found a pack of sanitary towels on my bed.

Despite the belly-aches and messiness of it all, I felt a sense of achievement and relief, as at ten years old, I was the last in my class to start my period. Maybe now I would be accepted by the girls?

As an adult writing this now, I look back at the pattern of precocious bleeding of all the pre-teen girls in my area and wonder if the talk of hormones in the milk at the time wasn't just a rumour.

20

Uncle Stephen and the Secret

Uncle Stephen is my favourite uncle. He is so much fun. He's always ready to play with me and he doesn't seem to take life too seriously like most grown-ups do. He's not like the other adults who are boring. We like the same pop music and our favourite song at the minute is Tiger Feet by Mud. We sing along and do the silly dance together. Not only that, but he's a fireman and every so often he takes me to the Fire Station (he's the Chief!) and shows me around. He's also silly like me and makes everyone laugh, especially when he plays the Pantomime Dame in the end of year Fire Station Christmas show. He looks so funny with his balloon boobies, he loves dressing up, just like me.

His wife, Aunty Heather, is quiet and a bit like a mouse. I'm much taller than her and noisier (and I'm quiet!). She doesn't say much but she likes to help me do my colouring in and she's excellent at it. They have a lovely dog who likes to play with my dog, Jemma.

Uncle Stephen has started visiting us regularly at the weekend. I like it. Sometimes he goes out with Dad and they come back a bit drunk but other times, he babysits me while Mummy is busy cleaning or ironing (she does that the whole weekend) and we go on 100 miles per hour drives down the motorway in his royal blue with white roof, Rover P6 car. That is so fast! Are you even allowed to drive that fast? It feels naughty, but such fun. I love the smell of the leather seats inside the car and the swirly, shiny, smooth wooden dashboard. I don't know whether I'm scared or excited, maybe both? I've never gone this fast in a car before. It gives me the same wobbly feeling in my belly that I get when I look at boys. Uncle Steve is so much fun! After our naughty escapades, we go to the chip shop and get chips and curry sauce. On the drive back home (not at 100mph), he always tells me not to tell my mum as she'd be cross with him so this was to be our little fun secret. Obviously I'm not going to tell her as my mum gets so mad over the stupidest things. ALL THE TIME.

I'd never want to get Uncle Stephen into trouble.

21

Strikes, Candlelit Baths, DDT & Teasing Witches

Just lately, we've had no electricity for days at a time.
Mummy says it's something to do with the government being rubbish and trade unions, whatever they are.

It doesn't make much sense to be because my dad works for the electricity board, why can't he just fix it? Anyway, I don't mind too much, it's a bit like camping, but with no horrid insects.

When we went camping in Wales, I had an important job. We all hated creepy-crawlies, well everyone except Dad that is. When you sleep in a tent you have to lie down on the ground where the insects live so Mum put me in charge of the 'puffer'. It said DDT on the white plastic cone and I had to pump it and puff out this nice smelling white powder that kept insects away. I would puff a line of this DDT powder all around the edges of the tent. I would puff it extra hard so I could breathe in the lovely smell.

So camping at home is fun because I love sleeping in my own bed and I love having a bath with candles. It feels so good to have the twinkly flames to stare into when I'm soaking in the warm water. I hate it when Mum puts bubble bath in the water first though. She thinks she's doing me a favour but I can't bring myself to tell her I hate it. The feel of the bubbles popping against my skin as I lay back on the end of the bath gives me the shivers. It's so disgusting. So I will put a bar of soap in the water to kill off the demon bubbles. Die, demon bubbles, die!

Mum has been moaning a lot recently. She spent quite a lot of time in bed and Dad sent for the doctor as he didn't know what was wrong with her. The doctor gave her some pills and said she was depressed.

Dad has started to go out to the pub with Uncle Steve regularly these days and comes back wanting slobbery, stinky kisses. He's always very silly when he's drunk but I don't like how it makes me feel. It feels scary and I don't know why. The other day Dad gave me a Chinese burn on my wrist and it really hurt. He thought it was funny, but I couldn't see why it was. Dad sometimes squeezes my knee at a certain spot and it feels like a jolt of electricity is going through my leg. I hate that but Dad thinks that's funny too. I think something's wrong with Dad's sense of humour. The other day he told me he had something for me and said to close my eyes and open my hand. So I did. He put a spider in my hand. He thought it was really funny when I ran away screaming and crying. That's not funny, not funny at all. Funny is when you both laugh, not one person laughs and one person cries.

Last night I had the dream again, the one about the witch. I've had it so many times now and it's always the same.
The witch ties me up to a post in the side garden, just below where the landing window overlooks it. Mummy is cleaning the landing window looking straight at me, while the witch starts to light a fire under my feet. I scream but nothing comes out of my mouth, and Mummy just smiles, waves at me and cleans the window.
I hate this dream! Why does Mummy never save me and why does she smile?

22

Porn, Santa, & the Man in the Window

Weird, Mummy is in a bad mood (actually that bit's not weird haha) but she's got all of Daddy's dirty magazines down from the top of his wardrobe. She's ripping them up and burning them all in the fireplace.

She's saying, "I'm not letting the bin men have these!"

Rude. I'm not supposed to know what these magazines are but I've been secretly looking at the pictures of the naked ladies for quite some time now, usually when Mummy and Daddy go out shopping. If they didn't want me to reach them, why is there a chair there, right next to the wardrobe, perfect for climbing on? They must think I'm a baby or something?

Just like when they hide the Christmas presents in the wardrobe, as if I don't know. Every year, when they are out of the house, I carefully unwrap the gifts and see what they are. Then I wrap them back up again and put on a pretend surprised face on Christmas morning when I unwrap them again. I think they forget I'm a clever girl. I also HATE surprises.

When I was little, they used to all laugh at me when I shouted thank- you to Santa up the chimney, for bringing me my presents. It made me very cross. I was just being polite like Mummy had taught me to be. There was no need to laugh at me. That felt horrid, it felt like they were mocking me.

Now, obviously I know that they were all lying to me about Santa. Santa didn't bring the presents, it was all Mummy and Daddy pretending. So I didn't feel guilty to lying to them on Christmas morning because they had lied to me first. That was just fair.

The man in the house across the back garden is staring at me through our kitchen window. He's standing at his kitchen window without a top on and doing something with his hand. He's making me feel weird.

Scared to tell Mum though.

23

Leaving On a Jet Plane

No! No! No! Mummy has just told me that we are moving house. Bad, bad idea! Even worse, we are moving country!

The only thing that stops me from completely losing the plot is that we are going to Africa. Mum says Daddy has a new job there and we are going to go and live in the sunshine.

At least I'll be able to see lions, I love lions.

The sad thing is I'll have to leave my darling doggy Jemma behind. She's going to go and live with Nan.

Urgh! I've just realised I'm not going to see Nan! That's bad. That's terrible!

Mummy's told me I'm to pack my favourite toy, just one as there's not much space on the aeroplane.

How am I going to choose and how will I explain to my dollies that they can't come?

It's going to have to be Teddy. I can't bear to leave him behind.

Ha! Ha! I made a word joke... but no, it's not funny. It's not funny at all.

I don't want to go.
But Lions and Tigers and Bears, Oh my!

Also, Diane, be real. You don't have a choice. You may as well be a suitcase they are taking with them.

The local newspaper is here and they want to take our photograph in front of our house. We are famous!
Local Notts family make a new life for themselves in South Africa it reads.

I got to wear my skinny polo-neck jumper and my favourite jeans this time. I smiled my best smile (I think?) It is always weird to smile on demand. Do you show your teeth or just squish up your cheeks? They took the photograph, my Dad with a lit cigarette in his hand, as usual. What does air even smell like without cigarette smoke?

I've been writing on Mum and Dad's cigarette packets ever since I learned to read and saw the warnings on the packs saying smoking kills. I don't want them to die and they just won't listen to me. So I keep writing ,
"Please don't smoke this!" and "Please don't, you will die! " with my red felt pen on their cigarette packets.
But nothing works. Maybe they want to die? Or maybe they just don't care about me?
They smoke so much, that they even drove all the way from Mansfield to the headquarters of John Player Special in London to cash in their loyalty coupons. They had hundreds of coupons, all bundled up and held together with elastic bands. They never showed me what they got but it was still fun to go to London and drive past Buckingham Palace. Even though Dad drove round and round the roundabout with Mum shouting at him because he didn't know where he was going.

Buckingham Palace was a bit of a disappointment really, if I'm honest. I thought it would be more like a Disney castle since the Queen lived there, but it looked more like an iced white flat box cake with a fence around it.

I love Disney, although Snow White's wicked Step-mum scares me. Aristocats is my favourite film because I have the record of the soundtrack so I can sing the film word for word, and it feels nice to know what is coming up next. Safe.

I want a Prince to come and rescue me and save me from being taken on an aeroplane. So when I go to bed, I spread my blonde hair out on the pillow like a golden halo, just in case Prince Charming arrives in the dead of night to whisk me away on his white horse. Then I lie in the dark with my eyes shut looking at the swirly bubble patterns inside my eyelids, and it feels like I'm lying on a cold, hard cloud. I know that sounds weird, but it feels nice.

Well Prince Charming didn't come, did he? So now we are all packed and off to say goodbye to Nan.

I don't want to cry but I do. Nothing feels right, right now. My grumpy Granddad is driving us to the airport in his Landrover so I get to sit in the back in the bit that has no seats, which is quite exciting. It feels naughty. Mum and Dad get to sit in the front with Granddad and I get to look after the suitcases in the back. It's an important job (apparently).

All the way to London I waved to the cars behind us. It's fun to be noticed and it turned into a game that helps distract me from what is happening. I feel carsick as usual, but I have a plastic bag in case of accidents. I was way too embarrassed to use it so I focused hard on the drivers of the cars behind us, then before you knew it, we had arrived at the airport.

I'm walking down the inside of a big, fat, silver snake and when I get to the end I'll be on an actual aeroplane for the very first time. I'm actually a bit excited now and my tummy wiggles are back.

I didn't like take-off. It was scary and hurt my ears, but now we are up above the clouds, it's cool!

Some strange man just offered me a cigarette! I told him I don't smoke thank you very much. Can't he see I'm ten, well almost eleven? In fact when we get to South Africa, I'll have my eleventh birthday after a few days.

I've grown quite tall, in fact I was the tallest in the class at school, at 5 ft 4 and the teacher worked out a graph that said if I kept on growing at this rate, I'd be a giant when I'm a grown-up. I better stop growing soon because that is just **not** happening. My legs are definitely stretching because I get horrid growing pains in my knees at night. My daddy will always get out of bed and massage my knee cramps away for me when he hears me crying. It always helps. I'm bendy like Daddy. We can both curl our fingers up like a Thai dancer, and press our thumbs back to meet our wrists. It's a cool party trick.

May 1975
After the longest, scariest plane ride of my life (well, it's my first time), we've landed in Africa!
South Africa,

Cape Town,
Jan Van Riebeeck airport.
The World
The Universe.

Well, honestly I must look really ancient, must be my boobs, because I just can't get over that man offering me a cigarette. Do you know, just before we left, Mum managed to get me into an AA movie (a 15) so I must look grown up for sure. It was Stardust, with the yummy David Essex. Mum did my hair fancy and put make-up on me. That was so funny. She was a bit weird with me after the film because it was full of F words and S- E- X. I think she was a bit embarrassed or something? I loved it though.

Part 3 Munchkinland

Where are the lions?

We are getting into a car and being driven to the house of a friend of my dad's. He lives in a place called Durbanville which is about an hours drive away. We will be staying with them temporarily until my dad finds us somewhere else to live. Mum says it shouldn't take too long, I hope that is true as I hate staying with people I don't know. This drive is taking long on this motorway in the dark. I strain my eyes against the passenger window to try and make out what I can see in the darkness outside. I still can't quite believe I'm in Africa!

What? I just saw something that looks rather like a fish and chip shop! That can't be right? Aren't we in Africa? Where are the lions?

The people we are staying with are very nice. They live in a cute, brand new build house sort of in the countryside. The houses are reallly far apart from one another. There are lots of tall trees that rustle in the wind called gum trees and the sky is bright blue in the daytime. It's quite hot, even though this is the South African winter, so I'm glad I've got my new blue and yellow dress to wear that matches my new shoes.

When I went exploring today I found a gecko in their back yard, which is type of cute lizard with big round eyes and fat toes. The funniest thing is, they lose their tails if they get scared, so I called him Tayloff. Get it?

Last night, the first night we got here, it was really difficult to sleep. I kept thinking about the tsongololas all over the tiles and bathtub. Tsongololas are shiny, black worm things with lots of tiny legs.

I think the English name for them is millipedes. Where is my DDT puffer when I need it? I think I prefer lions.

Anyway I got into bed after seeing these mini-monsters all over the bathroom and my legs started to itch and crawl as if I was covered with hundreds of tsongololas. I was so tired and restless that all I could think to do was to tightly wrap bath towels around my legs to stop the itching and reassure my brain that no millipedes could get past the barrier. After that horrendous night, I truly wish I was back in England!

24

An English Girl in Africa

Just like Dorothy in the Wizard of Oz, as a preteen, I went from the grey Midlands to the intensity of South Africa, swept along in the turbulence of a marriage in crisis.

I stepped off the aeroplane, like Dorothy stepping out of her crash-landed house, into a whole bright and new Technicolour world. This was a place where the sun shone brighter, the wind blew harder and the colours dazzled my eyes. Even the flowers were bigger (like the prehistoric looking Protea) and nothing felt real. I longed for the daisies and buttercups, cowslips and bluebells, violets and dandelion clocks and their sunshine bright flowers, poppies and pansies, snowdrops and daffodils (and let's not forget the roses) that I had left behind. These fragile beauties that grew in the temperate climes of Northern Europe would call out to me for the next eleven years, their sweet song, like a siren's call as I navigated along my own personal yellow brick road on a quest to return home. On that convoluted journey, I would meet the brainless, the heartless, the cowardly and courageous, just like Dorothy. Here I was, an eleven year old ingenue, in a strange new country that I was forced to adapt to and adopt as my new home.

My first, most unsettling thought as I was driven along a long motorway as we headed for our first place to rest, was *'This doesn't feel like Africa.'* It felt strange, shiny. There were shops that looked the same as English ones. My eyes couldn't find the difference they sought as they surveyed the built-up landscape that was mid 70s Cape Town. The extraordinary, imposing, breathtaking, majestic beauty of the flat-topped Table Mountain pulling us towards the city would be my only chink of access to the authenticity of this very inauthentic place.

What I think my body was sensing at that point was the invisible but overwhelmingly dark presence of apartheid, the political system of separation of races that was rooted in colonialism since the Dutch colonisers landed in 1652. These European settlers created their own version of Africa, an illusion of Africa seen through their European mindset, manipulating, dominating and enslaving the Indigenous population, ultimately creating a new language, Afrikaans, that began as kitchen Dutch, being a corruption of the Dutch language spoken by the domestic staff. This would go on to become the language and form the basis of the identity of the Afrikaner oppressor. A sense of supremacy would grow around the establishment of this new language, leading to apartheid laws in the 1940s after racial segregation was implemented in 1910.

As a child with fresh, innocent eyes, I first noticed a feeling of something not being right, a sense of things not being real, combined with a certain feeling of precariousness. I would find myself holding my breath, pinching myself, trying to wake myself up from this menacingly Technicolour nightmare dreamscape. The physical beauty of the land was undeniable. It would have been heaven on earth if not for this... feeling.

At the time, no-one had explained apartheid to me. There was no Google search I could turn to. I was deposited in this new place that was sunny and windy and unsettling.

Then I noticed them.
The signs.
WHITES ONLY/SLEGS BLANKES
They were everywhere, on park benches, on beaches, in public communal spaces, on buses, in libraries, in cinemas, there was no avoiding them. Then things started to fit together to paint a fuller picture of the ominous presence I was feeling. Why does everyone I see around me in Cape Town appear to be white?

Of course, growing up in the Midlands in the 60s and 70's I'd absorbed the racist propaganda of African savagery and poverty. It was a common occurrence for Mum to say " Think of the starving kids in Africa" to encourage me to eat my brussel sprouts. (It didn't ever work). Our only ideas of Africa came from deeply racist 'cannibal' films that used blacked up white people to portray African savagery, cooking white missionaries in cooking pots. The extent of this deliberate racist brainwashing makes me shudder. The most 'positive" imagery came in the form of charity appeals, using the white saviour trope to try and raise cash by showing how pitiful African children were, particularly in war zones or areas affected by famine. So little wonder really that my Paternal grandmother had asked my mother why she wanted to go and live in South Africa when there were all those (racial slurs) living there? Mansfield at that time, hosted the headquarters of the National Front, and clearly my family weren't immune to its poison. I won't say I don't see colour, as that is a statement of ignorance and privilege, but racism has never made any sense to me. It is simply not logical to discriminate and pass sweeping judgements on someone simply because of the amount of melanin in their skin, or texture of their hair. The external presentation of a human has always been secondary to me. I suppose, like my disdain for small talk, I seek depth in my knowledge and understanding of another human.

Once it became clear that the weirdness I was feeling was the absence of the very humans who should have been populating the land I had come to live in, I started to look for them. I soon found them, in the kitchens, cooking and cleaning, in the streets at night, sweeping and emptying the bins. They were in white people's homes looking after children and other domestic duties, and on open-backed trucks being driven out to labouring jobs. They were down the mines and in the factories.Then on one of the drives out of Cape Town in the day time, towards the suburbs, I spotted the shanty towns. These were make-shift settlements of huts made from corrugated iron, with cooking facilities being an outdoor fire. This is where the working black people of Cape Town were living. This is how they disappeared them. Writing this now, I am aware of the shock in my body and the guilt of omission from being a white person living during these times, not having even the awareness to say anything about it , least of all do anything about it. I'm made aware as if for the very first time of the real horror of the situation. There's a sort of cognitive dissonance that white people in South Africa during those times, experienced. This is not to excuse them, however, but I think I also drank some of the Kool-aid when I was there, keeping me docile and under control. I believe I would've been a rebel if I'd have had any opportunity to mix with people other than white. The social and cultural set up was deliberately engineered to make this nigh on impossible (and also illegal). At art school, I did have one black male friend of a friend, whom I endeavoured to take with me to the cinema. We couldn't get past the security guard who simply said, " Slegs Blankes." (Whites only). Of course this all sounds as if I'm making excuses for not fighting the system that I had found myself in. Realistically, I was already struggling to fight the enemy within, my mother, who had proven to be a tricky character especially as I reached puberty.

Maybe I do feel guilty, but I was so busy being a teenager.

While I was there, during the State of Emergency the police had powers to detain anyone for an indefinite time, without informing anyone, for any reason. I discovered years later, that one of the housemates in our shared accommodation, was working for the Secret Police. It was a strange, frightening and unpredictable time and place to be young and foolish.

The State of Emergency, in 1985, gave the South African President powers to rule by decree, heightening the powers of the military and police. Newspapers were heavily censored, they had blank pages inside the covers. Books and music had already been extensively censored, if viewed as vaguely 'communist' which in South African terms meant left-leaning. Terrible violence erupted in the Shanty towns as the military rolled in menacingly, in their yellow military tank- style vehicles. People turned on one another in desperation and fear, and a particularly horrifying punishment for being found a traitor to the cause, was 'necklacing' where a rubber tyre was placed around the victim's neck and set alight.

During this terrible time, I was working as a Scenic Artist at Cape Performing Arts, Cape Town's cultural centre. My job was painting theatrical scenic backdrops in large workshops. During this time, I had made friends with the black cleaning guy called Jeremiah. All of us scenic artists were issued hand- made tool boxes, made by the on site carpenters, to keep all of our heavy tools safe on the premises. At this time of unrest, our toolboxes kept going missing. Jeremiah pulled me aside one day and admitted that he'd been taking them so he could keep his possessions safe as he dared not go back to the township where he normally resided, because of unrest and the threat of him being made a necklacing victim. He told me that he and his son, were secretly sleeping in people's gardens to keep themselves away from the hostile environment.

Deep breath out...

Later on that year when I announced to my workplace that I would be returning to the UK, Jeremiah pulled me aside once more. With tears in his eyes, he begged me to take his only son with me to the UK for a chance of a better life with me. It was challenging to have to explain to him that although I was white, I was actually poor, and I would be living with my dad when I returned until I found a way to make money. It didn't seem kind to explain to him how impossible it would have been to fulfil his request when it came to immigration without a passport into the UK. At that time, South African black people had no access to their own passports. How very cruel to enslave the indigenous population and then remove their ability to leave.

I look back at my time in South Africa with mixed emotions. South Africa politicised me. She gave me a love for African rhythms after I first heard and fell in love with the world reknown Marimba band Amampondo in the streets of Cape Town. I discovered my love for bright colour and African textile, and my deep love for the sea. She also introduced me to the dark side of humanity, politicised racism, deep Patriarchal oppression and it's tool of warfare, rape. I also met the Wizard of Oz, who turned out to be a terrified old white man, pushing levers and projecting fear out to the masses. I'm glad he's now been banished from this land.

It's going to take a long time for this beautiful country and it's people to heal after generational trauma visited upon it and them going back centuries.

At least it's the beginning of the healing process now and it looks far more like itself at long last.

25

Important Decisions and New Discoveries

Mum says we are moving int our new flat and it's near Dad's work. That's exciting, I hope I get my own room. I'm also starting at a new school. It's an Afrikaans school, Mum thinks that it will be good for me to learn this funny sounding language that they speak here. I don't like how it sounds.

I HATE THIS SCHOOL!

This is so unfair! Not only am I the new girl which is bad enough, but I've been put back a year because of the language thing, so I'm with kids younger than me. I don't understand a word they say here. I don't know how much longer I can do this. The day is broken up with bells, and we have to go from one class to another. All I can do to cope is follow behind someone and copy them because I can't follow any verbal instruction. If I follow someone who's playing up, then I end up getting into trouble too! This is hell. I end up a crying mess at every home time, I can't help it. I'm so unhappy.

At least my teacher is nice. She speaks English to me sometimes. She's asked me to sew her a big soft toy frog that she brought in the pattern for. I think it's because I told her I'm good at sewing. That's because I've watched my mum on her machine for so long, I sort of just picked it up.

The toy frog came out really well and I was so proud to take it in to give to my teacher. At last I can do something properly! She's asked me to make another toy though. Hmm. Why is she doing this?

The assemblies in the school are just horrid and strange. We have to march into the hall like soldiers, I'm not joking! We are like an army, with swinging arms and everything, then they raise a South African flag and we have to sing the National Anthem, in Afrikaans of course. It all feels so alien when I think about my nice school back in England where we could be free and the teachers were kind and not making us march like soldiers. I'm not learning anything here either, (except how to make soft toys) so being here is pointless.

Mum's noticed how sad I am. It's hard not to miss it really. I cry every day.

Mum went for a meeting at the school and now she tells me I'm going to go to an English speaking school instead! Thank you!

One thing that I would do to cheer myself up a bit after school was to put on my nicest clothes and go walking on the bridge that goes across the motorway across from my flat. I've noticed that since my boobs have grown bigger (I'm a 36 B now!) men are looking at me, and every so often they would flash their lights or toot their horns at me if they were in the car by themselves. It was a delicious feeling, similar to the feeling I got on the way to the airport in the back of Granddad's Landrover. It's really exciting to be noticed. It feels grown-up. How did I go from Little -Miss- Invisible to Little -Miss -Stopping-Traffic? The attention gives me a tickle in my tummy. I like that. I want more.

Mum and Dad still fight. A lot actually. The other day they had a fight in the car when I was in the back seat and Dad started driving really fast. They were arguing about their friends who lived across the road, Bob and Eileen. Dad said Mum was cheating on him again.
I don't know, I don't care.
Just stop shouting!

I got so scared because Dad was driving on a mountain pass with a sheer drop and tight corners and it just felt so dangerous. I think I may even have asked God to help me. Even though I don't really believe in God but that shows just how scared I was.

Mum told me last night that she and Dad were getting a divorce. I don't know what to think, really. I hate that they fight all the time so I'm glad that they won't be doing that anymore. Then Mum said that the Judge who is doing the divorce needs me to choose who I wanted to live with. She gave me a week to decide.

The week is up and I've made my decision.
Even though I'm petrified to tell Mum, I've decided I want to live with Dad. He's always been kind to me, (apart from the insects thing, that is) and Mum, well she's Mum. Good at sewing and stuff, but can be scary, often.

So I told Mum.

That
    didn't
        go
            well.

"YOU BITCH! You are going to live with me whether you like it or not, you ungrateful bitch! " she screamed and slapped me across the face with such force that I flew across the room, landing in crumpled heap against the wall.

Shocked, hurt, confused and scared, I wondered why Mum had even bothered to ask me to choose in the first place.

26

The Body Holds on to Unkind Words

I'm lying face down, face pressed into the close embrace of towel and sponge.

I'm on a massage table receiving an aromatherapy healing session from my good friend, Sakli. This one is the second in two months. The first one had been a painful, dramatic affair, where she had cajoled and squeezed out deep-seated trauma that had been lodged for who knows how long in my right hand side (the masculine). The release had come with guttural, demonic sounding growls, mocking laughter, howls and a lot of sobbing. It was not what I was expecting from a simple massage and it astonished me. The resulting puddle of mucus on the floor under my exposed face being a rather disgusting souvenir and physical manifestation of trauma release.

This second massage felt different. It was quieter, certainly not as painful, even though I was curiously observing that Sakli was using the same amount of pressure as the first time. I expected to have to breathe through the pain but I stayed breathing steadily and calmly and focused in on my body sensations and any arising memories. All was calm and quiet except I found myself muttering,

" It doesn't hurt anymore" , which quickly turned into " You can't hurt me anymore." which I observed interestedly, at a distance as if I were another person in the room observing my massage. Nothing dramatic issued from my right hand side and I settled back into the massage thinking that this was going to be a calm journey. Then Sakli pressed into the area between my left forearm and thumb and I shouted out loud,

" YOU BITCH!"

I hastily reassured Sakli that that dramatic outburst wasn't directed at her, but were the exact words that my mother had used towards me when slapping me, over 47 years ago, when I had chosen to live with Dad and not her. What followed that initial profanity was my inner child's voice who sobbed and repeated over and over, just how terrified she was of her Mummy.

"I'm scared of you, Mummy, go away!"

Then the final utterance, filled with pathos,

"But I still love you, Mummy."

I marvel that my body had held on to this pain memory for so many years, almost half a century! I'd completed hours and hours of talking therapy during a three year stint of counselling training, but that never got near to the root of this pain like this body work just had.

The space between the elbow and the thumb I've come to learn is the grief meridian. Due to my mother's complex personality and my not being able to attend any funeral, I had not been able to grieve her loss. The death of a narcissistic parent often feels initially like relief to their adult children. This does not mean that their inner children do not miss their mothers.

I've forgiven my mother's actions since her passing. She couldn't have possibly lifted the lid on her Pandora's Box of trauma without severe threat of overwhelming the system, hence her inability to explore her pain and heal. Instead she chose to shut it all down with dissociation and prescription pills. It must have felt horrendous to have been separated permanently from your own sense of self. I can't imagine not ever having access to my inner world and my higher self. No wonder mum was so intent on crushing me, I represented everything she could never be, but wanted to be: comfortable in my own skin, letting go of judgement of others, enjoying a loving relationship with my children and grandchildren, allowing myself to be messy and fail without feeling hopeless, following my joy and living without fear.

None of these things were possible for her.

I'm sorry, Mum.

27

You say Goodbye, I say Hello!

I visit Dad every weekend at his very cosy wooden house. We cry all the time together, and play in the woods outside his house and go for long walks when Dad would sing Frank Sinatra songs. He has a beautiful singing voice. I wish I'd heard him singing when I was younger. I wonder why he never sang around Mum? We make dens, build forts and make fires and barbecue. It's called a braai in South Africa. When we go inside, Dad plays Elton John and Queen and of course we both sing some more.

When mum comes to pick me up, she scowls and looks angry because both Dad and I hold on to one another like monkeys and sob when we are forced to say goodbye.

Mum says we are soppy.

I hate leaving Dad on his own. It's not fair.

Mum says she has some good news, Nan is coming over on a big boat from England to live with us. We will be moving into a new house soon and Nan will be looking after me while Mum is at work. Good news at last! I've really missed my Nan and her pillows.

I'm now 12 and my new school is miles better although I'm only going to be here for a year and then I go to secondary school when I'm 13. Ugh, I seem to be constantly changing schools. I've made a friend called Zia, she's quite posh and I go to her house after school until Mum picks me up after work. Then we go home to Nan. It's been really nice having Nan back. She gives me lovely, squishy cuddles and cooks all my favourite food. She told me that I've been sleep-walking and talking recently and the other night she had to stop me from walking out of the front door in my pyjamas! What the heck!

Mum has put an advert in the newspaper for a boyfriend. She's getting loads of letters back from all sorts of men. She takes me with her when she meets them on the first date. It's very awkward most of the time, as some of them are creepy and yuck. I liked one of the men though. He was youngish and lived and worked in a lighthouse. We spent a fun day on the beach playing, but mum didn't like that one. I think he got on with me better than her. Ha!

Then there was a scary man who lived in the poshest part of Cape Town. Mum said it was like Millionaire's Row. She took me along on that date too, to that man's house. Well, more like his grounds. We never made it inside the house. He bought us tea out in the garden, in chipped tea cups while the peacocks strutted around us haughtily and screeched. They were beautiful to look at but terrifying up close, a bit like Mum. This man was a walking Scottish stereotype, he was ginger, old and mean. Even though my mum was still young and beautiful, even she couldn't melt this man's stone cold heart. Thank goodness though. I'd hate him to be my step-dad. You can keep your money.

Mum has been seeing an old Afrikaans man called Hennie. He's another of the men who wrote to her. He's got false teeth, yuck. She seems to like him though and he's often around. He looks severe and is very quiet and serious.

What the actual heck? Mum is getting married to Hennie and we are moving house again! To his house on the slopes of Table Mountain, in a place called Oranjezicht. It's quite posh. Nan is moving in with us too. She gets on well with Hennie so that's great.

Turns out Hennie is quite nice after all. He took me ice-skating which I thought was very brave of him. It actually might be nice having a kind step-dad , especially now that my Dad has gone back to England. I think I can get over the false teeth thing.

Part 4 A Story Within a Story

I Never Wanted You To Be Sally Bowles

"I'm sorry, please forgive me, I love you, thank you."

Here I am chanting the familiar Hawaiian prayer of the Ho'Oponopono,

"I'm sorry, please forgive me, I love you, thank you."

Over and over, I chant these magical, mystical words as I watch the large piece of paper with a man's name written on it get gradually consumed by the flames. Ignited by a stick of Palo Santo, the scent of the fragrant wood adding a touch of sweetness to this releasing ritual. Gradually, I watch as the paper greys, curls and dances into crispy ash, taking the name with it, releasing it and its hold over my energy into the chimney above. As I sit down to write and ponder how today I came to write a chapter that started almost half a century ago, I sigh. I still feel the echoes of an inner quiver, the remnant of my dysregulated nervous system, as earlier, I had been taken on an unexpected trip down memory lane.

I believe I was guided in some way. For a week or so, I'd been in a state of stillness. It's that strange limbo time twixt Christmas and New Year, made even more pointed now by the constant reminder of Imogen's eternal 28th birthday on New Year's Eve and this year would mark her eighth death day. I'm no longer a wretched mess in my grief state although it can still catch me unawares sometimes like a child in a white sheet, pretending to be a ghost, jumping out and shouting BOO! These moments are thankfully further and further apart. Now I'm much more aware of her presence manifesting as strong, full-body goosebumps, rather than her absence. She seems still, quite keen to be around.

It was after a good clear out prompted by the New Moon recently that I rediscovered a gift that Imogen had given me many years ago. It was a large cinema poster of Liza Minnelli as Sally Bowles in Cabaret, my favourite musical of all time. Imogen knew my story of almost being Sally Bowles in the school play, a role that fate had cruelly stripped away from me. Imogen had a knack of knowing exactly what to gift me on my birthday and her hand-made cards were extraordinary.

She may not have been much of a hugger (except if it was from behind) or any other obvious displays of affection, but this demonstration of deep understanding of what brought me joy went a long way.

I stuck the now, rather raggedy-around-the-edges poster onto my bedroom door. It wasn't lost on me that I had stuck it to the same place that was Imogen's childhood bedroom, a place where she had predicted the Twin Towers incident a good year before it even happened. She had collaged a magazine photograph of these iconic structures and over the top, in ransom note style cut out letters she had spelled out

WATCH THIS SPACE!
None of us gave it a second thought until way after the tragic incident had occurred. One of Imogen's visiting friends had noticed it and flagged it as being not entirely appropriate? Maybe even a little distasteful?
We all gasped when we realised what had actually happened.

Imogen was a little freaked out and tore if off her door, throwing it in the bin.

This poster of Sally Bowles sat right on the spot where that Twin Towers prediction had been. I felt it could be leading me to something, but what?
Bored, frozen in stillness, I picked up my phone and idly typed a long forgotten name into Facebook search. What on earth had prompted me to do that, I wondered? I hadn't thought about this man in over forty years or more.

There he was, Jan, but barely recognisable. Time had not been kind to the man, nor his figure. You could probably say the same about me, to be fair. Time was a cruel mistress. If it hadn't been for the cover photograph of a younger him in his band, I may have scrolled away thinking I had the wrong person. But no, it definitely was him. I poked around on his page then I left it, not quite knowing why I had gone there in the first place.

To my horror, the next morning, a ping from my phone alerted me to the fact that I had received a new message. It was from Jan. Apparently, I'd followed his page, he'd received a notification telling him, and this was him responding. He was asking to chat. What should I do? I couldn't pretend I hadn't poked this bear, so I thought maybe I'd use the opportunity to fill in some gaps in my memory of around the time we knew one another. It also might be interesting to hear his story about our brief time together all those years ago, if he was willing to share. Perhaps also, he could help me clear up some confusion.

I've just turned 13 and I've started at a brand new high school. It's certainly a bit scary, but I've made a friend called Vivianne and she and I have already started our secret coded language so that we can talk about the boys. Oh, it's so exciting! There are so many hot boys to check out! There's that boy with the black hair and big dark eyes that we called Arabian Prince (AP), then a short, cute blonde boy with a funny voice (FV, for funny voice, ha ha!) Stared like crazy (SLC) Love very Much (LVM), we were experts at communicating in our secret code right in front of the very boys we were talking about. It was so thrilling. I'm not sure if they noticed us, though, but we really hoped they did.

What Vivianne doesn't know yet though, is that I have a secret boyfriend that I met in the holidays at the cinema. He has a car! He's so grown up. I don't know if he's noticed that I'm a kid as I didn't have my school uniform on in the cinema, duh! Anyway now he knows I"m at school and he doesn't seem to care. He says he's going to pick me up in his car after school and save me the long train ride home. Oh yeah, I forgot, we moved house AGAIN but now we live in the cutest house on the mountainside just across the road from the sea, in a place called Kalk Bay. It's an hour train ride to get into Cape Town for school, but it's worth it because I love my new home and I love my new school too. David, (that's his name, which is my Dad's name too which is a bit odd) said we can go and park up at the beach for a bit before he drops me home. Mum will never know, it's a bit like time travel. His car is weird though. It's a Ford Capri but it has a big bump on the bonnet, it looks like it's pregnant and about to spit out a baby car. David says it's because he put in a bigger engine to make it go faster. I prefer my pregnant story ha!

I've added Jan to WhatsApp. We are going to chat. I've no idea what will come from this, but here goes.

Me: This is a bit awkward for me as I don't have much recall about back then. It was 46 years ago. I just remember my mum being so angry with me and sending me to a convent.

Him: She had good reason to be angry.

Me: ...

Wait, hold on there, we've only just begun
To live...White lace and promises, a kiss for luck and we're on our way...
(Go AWAY Karen Carpenter)
Is he insinuating I did something wrong back then, something shameful? I could feel my blood pressure rising and the hackles on the back of my neck start to prickle. A wave of nausea washed over me.

Him: Are you married?
Me: Divorced, long time.
Him: Okay, me too. I am currently engaged but I doubt I shall ever marry her. Are you ready for my voice? Perhaps it will jog your memory a bit?

Me to myself: I have no feelings for you dude, calm down already. This is not Facebook dating or some romance scam.

I didn't respond once again. I wasn't sure how. Nothing could have prepared me for what was to come. All I knew at this point was my mature self had no attraction on any level to this 64 year old South African, Christian, corpulent, Trump supporter. We were literally worlds apart.

David has been picking me up from school regularly now. Hey, I've become quite popular as the other girls are impressed that I've got a real grown man boyfriend with a sports car. I haven't told any of them he's 36 though. Hmm. That feels a bit weird now I think about it as he's older than my dad, but he's just as good looking. I miss Dad. He's gone back to England now and doesn't really keep in touch. David always takes me to FishHoek beach as it's just around the corner from my home , we park in the car park, put the seats back and listen to his 8 track stereo. I love music so much but his taste is a bit off though. I wish he'd play some Talking Heads or Queen. He buys me ice-cream and my favourite chewing gum that my mum won't allow me to have, Stimorol. It's got something in it that makes my mouth all cold. And I've got a secret. Sshh! David has been showing me his... thing, down there. He calls it 'Torty'. I mean, who even gives their willies names? That's so daft. Is that a thing? He's taught me stuff to do with it. I have to have a lot of chewing gum to stop me wanting to throw up and I just can't think about him weeing... ugh. But I'm getting used to it now. The other day we even played with Torty on the beach, I don't think anyone saw? I hope not. He's told me not to tell anyone as I'd get into big trouble, so it's our secret.

David has told me he has to go away for three whole months on an army camp. Before he leaves, he says he's going to treat me to something special to remember him by when he's away. He told me not to worry as he'll write to me and that time will go fast and that I should wait for him.

I actually built up the courage to tell my mum the other day that I had a boyfriend and his name was David (like my Dad) and he was going to be going away on an army camp. She just sort of looked through me? Had she even heard me? Ah well, at least she wasn't mad for once.

School has been really fun. I'm doing really well here. I love the French lab and Mr Philips, the teacher, who looks a lot like Richard Burton, mum would fancy him! He's really nice. I like the way French feels in my mouth. It's so much nicer than horrid Afrikaans (that no-one in this school seems to like learning). I'd much prefer to study Xhosa instead but it's not an option.

Something embarrassing just happened. My mum came to the school and asked for a meeting with the headteacher. Afterwards I was told that I wasn't to do art because my mum had forbidden it, even though it was a compulsory subject. She had threatened to pull me out of the school if they refused. What? I love art. This is ridiculous. I draw all of the time (all over my textbooks, but don't tell anyone) and Hennie, my Step-dad says I'm good at it. I even painted my own mural on my bedroom wall at home, it's a red beach sunset with palm trees and a girl in black silhouette. It looks really cool. I'm really proud of how it turned out. Hennie is a good carpenter, and he made me a white Hollywood style dressing table with lights all around the mirror that looks so good against it.

Anyway after I was upset about flipping art class being banned, Mr Stander, the art teacher (he's nice too) called me over for a chat and told me that the headteacher and he had a plan for me. He told me he was going to give me one to one art class after school and I was to tell my mum that I was doing netball.

This was fantastic! Thank goodness I wasn't doing netball for real though. I hated it. I struggled getting my body to do what my brain was telling it to do. It would frustrate me no end.

So officially I was allowed to lie to my mum in order to further my art career! Whoop! Whoop!

As well as art, English was my favourite subject. Basically I love words and their potential as playthings. The English teacher is hot too and that really helps keep my attention. He's from England and is a sort of posh, scruffy farmer in a dead sexy way. He breaks rules all the time and makes English really exciting.

He always wears this really ugly, crumpled hessian tie, I find that a bit odd. He gave it to my pretty friend, Birgitta at the end of class today and asked her to iron it for him. Apparently he doesn't have electricity where he lives. He says he lives in a small farmhouse off-grid, and he has a flock of sheep! The farm is in Hout Bay and some of my classmates say they've been there and it's great fun. I hope I get to go there one day.

I've just joined a Facebook group for us old-timers to reminisce about our time spent at Cape Town High. There are some photos in the group that take me right back to that very significant year, the year that so much happened to my just turned fourteen-year-old self. Ah, look! There's the sexy farmer English teacher. Oh no, it appears he's recently died. Here are some photos of him back when I remembered him, photographs of young kids in the 70s surrounding this handsome beatnik teacher, planting trees together on the school grounds. They were filling the holes with manure brought in on the back of his open backed Landrover from his Hout Bay farm. I find myself a little conflicted over the outpouring of praise and love towards this popular and unconventional teacher. I'd heard whispers of a darker side to him that no-one seemed willing to speak about. I've know that one mustn't speak ill of the dead (apparently) but in my world, nuance, justice and truth are more important than social conventions.

    I did eventually make it to the farm. I'd been invited along with a group of ten or so other kids, all my age or slightly older. I remember it being a thrilling day of adventure and discovery. The farm began with a steep bank of grass, atop which sat his ramshackle stone farmhouse. Most notably and incongruously, a bathtub sat by itself, outside the house, exposed to the elements and to all onlookers. Teacher explained to us newcomers that that was a perfectly romantic way to bathe under the stars, and if you haven't tried it, you should. I remember wondering how anyone managed to preserve their dignity and stop anyone seeing them naked? Perhaps they wore bathing suits, I thought, but then dismissed because then how do you wash the smelly bits? I marked this as an experience too strange to partake in and one to be avoided at all costs. Nevertheless, it turned out to be a fascinating and wonderful day. Farmer teacher demonstrated how to shear a sheep with hand-clippers. The sheep got the worst end of this deal, as evidenced by the deep red blood that oozed through the wool after being nicked by the sharp scissors. Farmer teacher's voice tuned out in my head as I stared as the red blood turned the edges of the grey fleece a dirty pink.

    I wasn't allowed to stay over-night, unlike the other kids that were there. This was the deal that I had brokered with my parents to allow me to visit Farmer Teacher's farm. My parents were to pick me up as soon as the sun set. I didn't mind, I was grateful for the opportunity to have had this unique experience.

Looking back from my present perspective, it was the mid seventies, right slap bang in the middle of the Hippy zeitgeist. Our crazy English teacher had brought a version of flower power and eco-awareness to South Africa. But in amongst all of this peace, love and harmony, something felt a bit off.

Even though I had spent the day with several young teenagers, I had mainly kept myself to myself. I didn't really know the others well, and making friends didn't come easily for me. As the sun started to fall behind the mountainside and the evening drew near, we were all invited to sit in a circle and Teacher passed around a big glass bowl he called the Loving Cup. It contained a mysterious drink that we were all expected to share as a bonding ritual. They always did this at the end of the evening apparently. I cannot tell you what was in the Loving Cup as there was no way I was going to share spit drinking out of a communal cup. The thought disgusted me. So I passed when it came round to my turn.

Before I left, one of the girls, who was around my age, 13 or 14, came up to me and whispered that she had been chosen to spend the night with Teacher. I didn't know what to think or say. Was she joking? Was she lying? Who knows. But circumstantially, it doesn't look great. My gut knew something was not quite right and I was glad I was now headed home safe in my parents car.

Still, Teacher Farmer, whatever the truth was, you remained an inspirational teacher. Sleep well.

So today is the day! David is taking me somewhere special in his car after school. I've sneaked a change of clothes in my PE bag in case he takes me for a milkshake or something. I can't be seen in my school uniform out there with him, it's ugly and embarrassing. Instead of heading past my house like we usually do, he takes an early turn-off up Boyes Drive. My heart starts to beat faster. That's odd, there are no shops or restaurants up this way, just the mountainside. He drives quite a long way along this mountain pass road, the view of the False Bay coastline, a sheer drop on the right, the close hug of the rocky mountain face on the left. He reaches a viewing point with an empty car park area and pulls the car to a halt. No-one else is here. It is mid-week, mid-afternoon. He turns towards me after jerking up the handbrake, looks me slowly up and down and says in a weird, thick voice,

"I just want to make you happy."

David gets out of the car and walks over to my door. He opens my door as if he were going to let me out of the car, like a gentleman, but instead he pushes me roughly back against my seat and clambers his bulky body over mine. I freeze. I have no idea what he's trying to do. Then he squeezes himself into the footwell, pulls down my knickers and pushes his face in between my thighs. My heart is racing. It pinches. Ouch! It hurts, it's not nice, whatever he is doing. I don't like it at all. Stop! I shout, or at least I think I do. I'm not sure that any sound is coming out of my mouth. It's just like the witch dream all over again. It made no difference anyway as he just carried on doing whatever he was doing. Then finally he stops and pulls me out of the car, drags me over to a large rock face, pushes me up , face against the rock and him behind me, and then Torty hurts me in the place where the pinching was happening.

He's driving me home now.
I'm sitting silent like a statue in the front seat. I look down at the footwell where his body had been and I shiver.

When I get home I cry quietly in my bedroom so mum wont hear me. What had he just done to me? He said he wanted to make me happy so why do I feel so sad?
I feel so strange and floaty, like nothing is real and I feel dirty, very dirty.

I never saw him again, but I found a photo of a Ford Capri in a magazine that I stuck on my bedroom wall. I'm not sure why I did that.

28

How Not to Get Raped

I wasn't very old, perhaps I was ten? The details of precisely when evade me, but a memory of an encounter with my mother that has just popped into my head. She was showing me a book that she had borrowed from the library that she wanted me to read. It was called *How To Say No to a Rapist and Survive*.

I've just Googled it and found out that it was published in 1975, so my memory served me well. The book was written by Frederick Storaska. It is widely criticised today and I'm not at all surprised. This book left me permanently traumatised. Some of the advice to women in it was non-physical, and quite frankly, comically patronising, like feigning being pregnant, pretending to have a sexually transmitted disease, or actually vomiting on your attacker. I can't see any of these tactics deterring any rapist as far as I'm concerned. The advice is frankly, comical and potentially dangerous. It was the physical advice that had haunted me throughout my life after picking up this book.

It read thus:

Pretend you are going to romantically kiss your attacker. Slide your hands up his face in a caressing manner, thumbs inwards, then as you kiss him, quickly plunge your thumbs into his eyeballs, pushing his eyes deep into the sockets and into his brain, killing him instantly.

Yes, that took a dramatic turn didn't it? This imagined scene managed to sear itself into my brain and would create a trigger that would fling me out of cinemas if ever this scene was depicted in the film. I found out that it was used fairly often in many films, much to the detriment of my frazzled nervous system.

If there mere mention of this technique could affect me so badly, you can only imagine the damage that actually going ahead with this instruction would wreak. It would also result in a murder charge. We know Patriarchy protects rapists and punishes women. That's old news.

Wonderful advice there, man. Bravo.
I'd prefer if he'd have saved his energy and spent it on teaching men not to rape.

This book was the only 'conversation' mum and I had had about rape. It basically told me, don't get raped, and if you do, it's your fault for not applying the lessons in the book correctly. The biggest thing I learned from mum giving me this book to read was that mum carried a lot of fear around my getting raped at an early age.

After I had had a total nervous breakdown later on in life, and my mother had begged and pleaded with me via e-mail for me to tell her what was wrong from what I thought was the safe distance of South Africa, I made the mistake of thinking mum wanted to support me and had the capacity and empathy to do so. So I relented (more fool me) and told her that I was raped by a paedophile at the age of 13. I wish I had never told her, to this day, because what transpired would birth my Medusa rage and ultimately lead to my going no-contact with my mother a few months later.

HOW MEDUSA BECAME A MONSTER

Medusa was once considered to be a beautiful woman. She caught the lustful eye of the sea God, Poseidon, who raped her in the sacred temple of Athena, goddess of warfare and wisdom. Athena, furious at what she saw as the desecration of her temple, blamed Medusa for being raped, punishing her by turning her into the snake-haired Gorgon with a gaze that could turn anyone into stone.

A goddess of wisdom and warfare who would blame another woman for her own rape? That resonated with what had just happened to me. No wonder Medusa came to be my most important Protectress, along with Kali Ma and lately, Gaia. As usual, like in all Patriarchal systems, no-one held the perpetrator, Poseidon to account.

My mother's immediate reaction to my telling her I'd been raped at 13 was to call me a liar and an attention-seeker and a whore. She told me categorically that I had had no time to be raped. She had made sure of that. She had spoken to my step-dad who had confirmed that no, I had no time to be raped. It was all in my imagination and how very dare I hurt them with these twisted lies?

The pain I felt on receiving these words as I read my mother's accusatory e-mail, was like no other pain I had felt up to that point. My head swam as I felt compelled to try and prove to myself of the validity of my memories and experiences. I found myself frantically digging around in dusty folders for letters that my step-dad had written me during the time when Mum had first divorced him (she had since remarried him). In these letters, Hennie spoke of his worry around my mother's mental state and that she had had a nervous breakdown. Despite being recommended she get help by the resident psychiatrist at the local hospital, Mum had refused any form of help and so Hennie was left to manage her in her fragile mental state. See? I wasn't the only mad one in the family. Or was I? I needed the pain to stop.

I found myself donning clubbing gear, leaving the house and stopping off at the local off-license for a half bottle of vodka in a paper bag, and downing it in the back seat of the upper deck of the bus on my way to dance my blues away.

I needed to escape this... whatever this feeling was. By the time I arrived at the club, 20 minutes later, the vodka hadn't quite kicked in and I sailed confidently past the familiar girl on the door of my regular club. I would go dancing almost 6 nights a week during this turbulent time of my life. I know now that dancing helps regulate my nervous system. I'd always arrive early so that I could guarantee an empty dance-floor so it would just be me, the DJ and the music. I'd lose myself in the dance. Usually the dance was all the medicine I needed but this night, things were a bit different. This pain required much stronger painkillers.

The DJ recognised me immediately and gave this dancing fool a hug on arrival. I think he must have spotted then that I was a little worse for wear. I didn't normally drink when I danced and this night was going to be an exception. The vodka had caught up with me and the DJ started buying me beers, which was very out of character for him. After an hour or so, my world was quickly collapsing around me and a part of me knew I would need rescuing pretty fast.

So I called my latest romantic interest who had been very kind to me. He wasn't a drinker himself and could be pretty intolerant of drunkenness but I had no other options. I got through to him and remember just saying help. The music was loud and I couldn't hear his response so I hung up. Then my phone rang and it was someone I had been seeing casually, and he quickly heard that I was inebriated. He knew where I usually danced so he told me to stay where I was and he'd come and get me. He scooped me up from the club and took me home in his car, followed me up the stairs and if it was the most natural thing in the world, raped me on my sofa before leaving without saying goodbye. He hadn't even bothered to take his hat off the whole time and hadn't said a word to me throughout.

Then the man I had tried to call earlier called me and told me I'd called him numerous times and all he had heard was the music and me saying help. He had no idea where I was, nor what was happening, and had been frantic all night , trying to work out what was going on with me.

Good question. I wish I knew.

29

Chinese Party and the Pain.

I just had the best and worst 14th birthday party. It was Chinese themed because I wanted to wear the beautiful aqua blue satin robe that my dad's youngest brother, Uncle Richard, had brought back from his travels in the Navy for me.

It was so smooth, silky and shiny and felt so good against my skin. I look gorgeous in it too. I was going to make the BEST party ever that everyone would talk about. Mum got me loads of paper cups, plates and black permanent markers, and I got out my stack of library books that I'd borrowed for research for 'Operation Chinese Party'. I decorated each cup and plate by hand, meticulously copying Chinese characters on them with black permanent marker. It took ages but it was worth it. I'd decided on the menu: stir fry chicken and veg followed by a dramatic ice cream bombe for desert. The best thing was that my mum had allowed me to do it all by myself. The weather was fine so it was going to be set outside in the back garden and I had spent hours and hours making individual pink and white tissue paper cherry blossoms that I was going to festoon around the garden. When I finished, I was so proud of how everything looked. It looked magical. Mum strung up some fairy lights as a final touch and with a final reminder of ' No alcohol allowed!" the party officially began. My tummy was in knots. Would people turn up this time?

Well it started off okay. Plenty of people turned up and they looked like they were having the best time. About ten minutes into the party, I realised that I much preferred the preparation to hosting, but I slapped on my best smile and tried to be the life and soul of the party. It was after about two hours that things started to shift. The energy started to become much more frenetic and chaotic as more and more people turned up and I started to panic as I realised I didn't know many of the people who were coming in the back gate, and horror upon horror as I realised they were bringing in alcohol! I didn't know how to stop it and I got really scared of what Mum would do. I hid for a while in the little outdoor shed but listening to the growing cacophony, just made things worse. So I made my excuses and ran inside and locked myself in the toilet. That's when the pain began. I ended up stuck on the toilet for the rest of the party with massive stomach cramps. Eventually my stepdad got everyone to leave but I couldn't even say goodbye because I was in so much pain. The pain didn't go away even when everything had been tidied away. It kept going for another week and I couldn't even go into school. Mum got worried and took me off to see the doctor.

The doctor poked and prodded me and did embarrassing tests on me and my poo. He thought that I might have something called dysentery, but I didn't. In fact, the doctor couldn't find anything wrong with me at all. He finally said it was something called psychosomatic, which basically means he thinks I'm making it up. But I'm not! My belly cramps and it hurts a lot!

Something exiting happened at school today that helped me forget about my belly pain for a bit. I got a part in the school play! It's a musical called Cabaret and I've got the part of a prostitute called Fraulein Kost. I have a few lines to say and a whole song to sing by myself! I'm so proud of myself because I'm only in Year 6. There are adults in the play too, in fact the leading role of Sally Bowles is a semi-professional singer who I think must be someone's mum. I can't wait to be on stage. It's weird, I don't ever feel nervous on stage, in fact it feels natural for me. I can be a bit of a show-off when I want to be, even though I'm still really shy. I'm not sure how that works but that's me!

A girl in my class says her brother fancies me and that he is in Matric. His name is Jan. She says he might take me to the Matric dance if I'm lucky. She's going to be our go-between so we can swap letters to one another. That's fun, especially as David hasn't bothered to write to me from the army. It makes the day more exciting to have a secret pen-pal boyfriend. I don't even know what he looks like, but I don't care! He's in Matric, imagine, I might get to go to the Matric dance if I play my cards right.

30

Jan's First Voice Note

January 2025

'I'm afraid I'd forgotten about my sister being part of you and me. You wanted to go to the Matric Farewell, I didn't have a date for the evening because I wasn't involved with anybody and I was too shy to ask anyone in my own class, purely because I was not part of the in-crowd. I did my own thing. I was a loner. Although I had many friends at school, I didn't run in a crowd.

I had to get special permission to get you to come to the Matric dance, and it was approved. Then we went to the dance and I took you home.

Erm, I'm sorry I'm going to have to correct myself as I realise that there was a really important moment in my life that happened at school. I had to phone my parents to come and pick us up after the dance. I remember asking the Principal (do you remember that?) and he gave me the key to his office to use his phone. You and I went into his office. I phoned my parents and then I kissed you in the Principal's office. That was our first kiss and also a very special moment in my life because I don't think many guys get to kiss their girlfriend in the Principal's office. My parents then took you home.

You invited me over to your house the next day (I guess you don't remember that either?) and this is where it gets beautiful and weird. Erm, ja! It's how I remember it.
I don't know how to err... (giggles nervously) I'm blushing, okay? So, err... bear with me.
I arrived there , your parents were busy in the back garden braaiing, and you invited me back to your bedroom. You introduced me to Queen which is still, to this day, my favourite, favourite group. I learned to sing by listening to Freddie , I recorded a version of Bohemian Rhapsody. It's not as good as Freddie, but I didn't have the same recording facilities that he had.
Ja!
But err... we started kissing and err...(sighs deeply then blurts out loudly)
I got my first blow-job from a fourteen-year-old girl and I fell in love with you right then.

You were fourteen at the time and I was eighteen and we decided to be together. Still to this day, I accredit everything I know about making love, it came from you. We used to go up into the mountains, the caves, and we used to go down to Woolleys Beach and erm... we were like two little rabbits whenever we were together.
There was no way, if anybody looked at you, they would NEVER have said you were fourteen. We made love on the steps of the band's place on the beach at Muizenberg and some people walked past and caught us. But ja!
I guess you don't remember that either.

31

Fourteen year old journal entry

Who is the only girl from year 6 allowed to go to the Matric Dance then? Me!!

So Jan took me. I felt so grown-up.

It's funny though, I thought I'd enjoy it much more than I actually did.

It was a bit loud there. The teachers were all there, drinking and being weird, dancing and being silly. It made me feel a bit squirmy seeing them out of context. They were cringey and embarrassing, so I was glad when it was all over to be honest.

Maybe I just don't like parties, but everyone likes parties because parties are fun?

I dunno.

Here's a funny thing, though, Jan kissed me in the Principal's office and it was ... hmm, okay I suppose.

To be honest, between me and you, diary, I don't really fancy him much.

But I like having a boyfriend and David has disappeared so...Jan must be the new one I suppose.

32

Jan's Second Voice Note

The Creation of the Manic Pixie Dream-Girl

Ja! What can I say? You and I wrote letters to each other and we had our...

It wasn't only a physical attraction we had towards one another, we also had some kind of spiritual connection.

I used to ask you things over the phone, like what colour paper am I holding up?

I'm writing a letter to you, what colour paper am I writing on?

You'd tell me the colour of the paper every time.

Apart from that, there were things that showed me that we had some sort of ESP (extra-sensory perception) between us, which is why I said it was a beautiful but weird time.

But then I wanted to know more about YOU.

I wanted to know why it was that at fourteen years old, you were sexually active?

Then a story of a guy called Dave came out, Dave Victor, with a Capri Perana.

You had a photo of him in your room, of this Capri Perana, and that hurt me immensely because you didn't have a photo of me in your room but you had one of him!

JA!

That was extremely painful.

Somewhere along the line of our relationship, you had ample opportunity to sit me down and say, I'm going through something.

When you told me about David Victor, he was apparently your ex-boyfriend that you had this fling with and I kind of had to make peace with that. I had to deal with the extreme pain of it.

Still to this day I have that pain but I guess that is not going to phase you in any way, because you were

'just a child'.

You don't take responsibility for anything that you ever said or did!

You exonerate yourself from anything you have ever said or done or caused.

You are not prepared to admit that every time you ever said that you loved me, that every time you wrote it down on a piece of paper, it was a lie! For you, lying is just as good as telling the truth and I'm asking you to stop using the fact that you were a child.

Every bit of pleasure that you did, you enjoyed. You didn't only do things to please me, I would've picked that up. If I had any suspicions that you were lying to me...I've been lied to all my life, I know what a liar sounds like, you were not lying at that stage. I don't believe it and will never believe it, and JA!

You know that it's also narcissistic when you say it's not my problem so I'm not going to deal with it? Then you too have become a narcissist and I never before took you as a narcissist, never before in my life. If you were not the person that I took you for, I would never have been with you. I would never, 46 years later, try to help.

JA!

We were both children, BOTH children!

I was a little older than you, eighteen, but you were far more mature than I was.
You taught me about making love, you taught me about good taste in music, you taught me about Queen, about Paul Williams, so look beyond the excuses for whatever and stand up and say,
"You know what? I'm actually going to do my part in this, this time and stand and fix what I broke!"

33

Dear Diary, It's Me Again

Oh my god, it's a miracle! You won't believe what has just happened...
I've just been asked to be...
(drum roll please)
Fanfare...
SALLY BOWLES!
Pinch me, someone. Am I dreaming?

The woman who was going to play her, can't now because of something called vocal nodules. Anyway, her loss, my gain. Let me tell you how this happened, because if I tell you, dear Diary, I might just start to believe it's true!

I was practising my solo song at the piano at break-time, singing my little Fraulein Kost heart out, when out of the corner of my eye, I saw the director and my English teacher, whispering to one another and watching me.

They asked me to sing the title song, Cabaret. Well, I didn't need much encouragement, to be fair. I've been singing this song at home ever since I got the part of Fraulein Kost, because I love it so much. I don't really know what it's about but I just sort of feel it. So I gave it my best shot. Afterwards they told me I had the part! They said that even though I was just a Year 6, they felt I had the maturity and talent to hold the role. Get me! Most importantly,

I wouldn't suffer being taken out of class time to do the extra rehearsals required because apparently, I'm smart.

I'm ready, more than I have ever been. THIS IS EPIC!

Obviously Jan has left school now after the Matric dance, but he's continued to write to me everyday using his sister as the postal service. He's been coming over to my house every weekend and we've been...ssshh... doing it. Loads. Mum has no idea, she'd kill me if she knew. I even lied to her the other weekend and told her we were going to the Jewish museum and then to the cinema to see Sergeant Pepper's Lonely Hearts Club Band at the cinema just to give us some excuse to not be at home. (Why didn't I choose a film that I'd actually seen?) Anyway, Jan and I had the whole day planned out. We went to his brother's flat and I got soo drunk. I can't quite remember what I did, but I do know it was a lot of fun. It doesn't matter how drunk I get, I always seem to sober myself up before going home. I think it may be fear of the mother that does it. Ha! Anyway my mum didn't have a clue. Good job. I'm keeping all of Jan's letters to me under my mattress along with this journal. He writes about everything we do in great detail, I think I excite him quite a bit, teehee! I better hide them well.

My life is over.

I want to die.

In assembly this morning, my name was called over the tannoi system, in front of the whole school. I was told to pack my books and go straight home. I had no idea why. My mind raced on the hour- long train journey back home.

I was thinking about all the things it could be. My heart thumped in my chest and I could barely breathe.

When I got home, I was met at the front door by my Nan who was sobbing. She told me to go downstairs to the basement.

I found my stony-faced mum on the far side of the big desk in the basement. In front of her, opened and spread out on the desk where Jan's letters and my diary!

My life was surely over.

"Is this true?" barked Mum, staring coldly at me.

Of course I lied through my teeth and denied every written word, trying to hide in the security of fantasy.

Mum wasn't having any of it, she knew I was lying. The evidence was right there in front of her.

" I'm going to get him locked up for statutory rape! " she shouted.

My stomach lurched. I knew my mum meant business. I was terrified of what she might do to him. My whole body was in a panic as I pleaded for her to change her mind. Too late, she'd already called Jan's parents and put a stop to us continuing in the relationship.

I hoped Mum was bluffing when it came to the prison thing. I didn't mind particularly about her putting a stop to me seeing Jan, as I was starting to feel a bit worried about how serious Jan was becoming about me. I was starting to regret getting into a relationship with someone I didn't really fancy or love so in a way Mum had done me a favour. I didn't want him to go to jail though. That thought was terrifying.

Did I feel guilty for stringing Jan along? Not really. I know I'd told him I loved him and I wrote it in all the letters too, but wasn't that what boyfriend and girlfriends said to one another? It didn't mean much, did it? I mean, Mum always tells me she loves me but she's not very nice to me , so...Mostly it didn't feel fair that Jan would go to jail over something I started. I keep telling Mum that I started it, it wasn't his fault but she won't listen to me. I sobbed and pleaded with Mum to punish me instead and leave him alone because it was all my fault. She doesn't believe me.

I'm so frustrated.

She gave me an ultimatum: convent or boarding school. It was a no-brainer for me. I chose the convent as it was a 15 minute coastal walk down the road and right opposite the beach. I could be a day girl and I was to start the following week, suspiciously right in the middle of term. Yeah, not great for making friends.

Oh and bye bye, Auf Wiedersehen Sally Bowles.

34

Conversation with Jan, Aged 64

January 2025

Me: I was an groomed and abused, autistic child of a Narcissistic mother who had her own issues with promiscuity and adultery that I witnessed from a young age. I was groomed and raped by a paedophile at 13, that was the year that my dad left for England. I thought the paedophile hadn't noticed I was a child, despite him being at a children's matinee movie screening of Heidi, where he preyed on me. He didn't touch me for six months, then raped me after teaching him how to please him orally. I only understood he was a paedophile after a full breakdown when I was 36 (interesting pattern there) when I wrote memories down to try to hold on to reality and make sense of my life that was descending into chaos. The first thing I wrote was:

" I was 13, my boyfriend was 36."

These words seemed to punch through the fog and into my gut. Our brains do that, you know? They protect us from ourselves and overload of trauma until we are in a safe enough space to be able to process it.

That situation set me up for what happened between us. It wasn't love from me, as I had no real understanding of what love was. To me saying I love you was a learned behaviour, an expected social action when you were in a relationship. I didn't know that it was meant to come with any attached feeling. I know that may sound strange, but that is what I had learned from growing up with my mother. She used the words towards me all the time. She would tell me she loved me every day, yet they never came with any loving feeling. In fact, quite the opposite. I was an epic people-pleaser, survivor. My mum terrified me, it sounds bad but I felt relief when she died.

All the things I did with you, all the places we went, all the risky behaviour, were things and places I'd done and been with him. They were the same places he took me to and the same behaviours he'd groomed me into performing, so I acted out, again and again. I'm afraid you were part of the fallout of all this.

I'm sorry if I've just popped your bubble.

Him: Well for what it's worth, you were my world and I genuinely believed you loved me. There were times when you acted strange, but I wrote it off as you being you.

Me : The clues were all there.

Him: My bubble has been popped many times. I have no idea what love is now.

Me: When I was called out of school and it all blew up, I thought someone had died. I was terrified on the train journey home, that I do remember. Mum was screaming that she'd get you locked up and my Nan was sobbing. I was terrified you'd end up in jail.

Him: I'm sorry I put you through that. I was terrified too, but I also realised it was only threats. My dad did a lot of that to me too.

Me: I was living a double life, a secret life. I was living dangerously because I was so scared of Mum so unable to tell her what was going on with me. Because of the unhealed trauma from abuse, I continued to act out sexually, compulsively, but in even more dangerous ways. Even after you. Then it became sex with strangers.

Even when I was at the all-girls convent, I found time to feed my hunger, I made time. It was a compulsion and a need to be free. I put myself in situations where but for the grace of god, I could've died many times over and no-one would've known. I could have been part of the missing children statistics.

I got ill, my body, especially my womb-space was full of trauma. Doctors thought I was just making it up. So when I was cast as Sally Bowles, a woman who had a past full of trauma, I don't think the teachers knew just how fitting the role was for me. I WAS her. But of course, as you know I never got to play her.

I kind of still want to be her.

Him: I NEVER wanted you to be Sally Bowles. It killed me to know of your pain. To me, that wasn't you.

Except that you are a wonderful lover.

When we were in my brother's flat, do you know we used 13 condoms?

Curtain.

Tumultuous applause.

The audience files out. The house lights go down.

Sally Bowles enters the empty stage from behind the curtain and sits on the edge of the stage, swinging her torn, fish-net stockinged clad legs.
A spot light switches on to her face, the camera pans in to reveal that she is a young girl, around 14 years old under the thick pan make-up and false eyelash disguise. Fat tears plop onto the stage as she sits there crying. Then she says quietly:

" I'm sorry, I didn't mean to cause you any pain. Please forgive me for not loving you. Now please, just let me go. "

35

Boundaries

I've just dug around in a drawer for a folder I previously recalled seeing there.

I need a folder so I can organise the increasingly growing flurry of handwritten foolscap pages that is the becoming of this book. I need to organise the chaos before the chaos completely overwhelms me.

Boundaries, the things that I didn't understand as a child, I've finally managed to establish now as a 60 year old woman. It's never too late. I'd had the realisation, quite literally through my practice of dancing the 5 Rhythms, that freedom is only made possible by creating a safe container. Firm, well established, enforced rules, help my nervous system that is quick to flip into fight, flight, freeze mode, to regulate. Then I'm able to be safe enough to be my true, vulnerable, expressive, weird, fabulous unmasked self. In true paradoxical fashion, the rules have set me free. My subversive soul enjoys this.

Tiny NO dress sculpture by Julia Maddison

Inside the folder, I discovered notes and drawings that I'd previously never seen. This was clearly Imogen's old, school photography folder. The first thing that jumped out at me was her sketch of a bronze sculpture by an artist called Juan Manuez, labelled Hanging Figure, 2001, possible self-portrait, Death by Hanging. It was a hasty, yet expressively accurate sketch of this very disturbing sculpture, captured from two viewpoints. From immediately in front of the sculpture, the body viewed head on, the head thrown back and another from the side, the noose clearly bearing the weight of the body in both images.

I could feel my body start to tense and I realised I was holding my breath. The inner wobble started to rise up once more as it felt as if I had tapped into another strange time loop of Imogen predicting her own demise. Especially as I write this as it's only three days post her 8th death anniversary on New Year's Eve. This feels like another signpost for sure. Imogen had a dark sense of humour, this felt like another of her darkly humorous messages to me that I was on my path. The words I heard in my head were,

JUST KEEP GOING.

I found another piece of paper in the same file, clearly one of Imogen's study notes. It was a flow-chart explaining and exploring boundaries. The concept had been expertly dissected.

It explored how artists often challenge boundaries, social conventions and protocol. That certainly spoke directly to my younger self and my older, wiser mature artist-self. I felt a deep resonance here with my wounded inner child. She took so many risks. The more her mother tried to shut her down, put her behind bars and restrict her freedom, the more the drive for freedom would become in order to act on the compulsive acting out that was fuelling her every decision. I speculate that this behaviour may be tied to not having any safe place to explore what had just happened to her. Even her diary was no longer a safe option. She had no-one to turn to.

It would take over 46 years until she felt safe enough to start to unpack these feelings in the safe space created by her dear friend Sakli. On the massage table she would have the extraordinary insight that anywhere felt safer to little Diane than home, even if that was in the arms of a total stranger. That maybe her risky behaviours were a childish attempt to get her to be thrown out of home, so she could be away from the unpredictability of her mother.

I'm scared of you Mummy. But I still love you.

36

An Open Letter to Jan

Dear Jan, (not your real name but you should recognise yourself)
In case you ever read this book.

After our conversation on WhatsApp in early January, I'm truly sorry that I felt for my own safety, I had to block you and that meant, consequently you could never really get any closure from our interaction. I hope this letter helps remedy that.

I understand that my actions as a child were perplexing for you. Why wouldn't you have believed my words of love at that time? Anyone in your position would have felt the same and I can understand how deeply wounding it must have been to find out that those words were empty. I am deeply sorry for that.

A few years after we were split up, I heard through the grapevine that you'd subsequently joined a church and I was being spoken about as a "Jezebel "and demonic spirit that had corrupted you. In your broken-hearted, confused state, I can appreciate how powerful and seductive a reframe this must have been for you. It would have helped you with a place to put your pain and anger. Now looking back at my life, I'm able to understand that 14 year-old me was just doing what she thought everyone did under those circumstances. I can understand, and I acknowledge that this would have been received as lies and deception and for that, I can only apologise now for hurting you. I don't know the circumstances in your life that caused you to be trapped, fixating and searching for another version of 14 year-old me. That must have been very frustrating and unfulfilling for you especially as the very thing you were looking for was just an illusion. The 14 year-old me was incapable of emotional maturity for obvious reasons. However due to the complexity of how the impact of child sex abuse manifests, my body was able seek out and enjoy physical pleasure, not understanding the toll it would take on my psyche many years down the line.

When you told me you had every intention of marrying the first person you ever had sex with, that scared me. You clearly meant me. I wonder if you'd ever factored in my part in this decision? This level of obsession and what to me felt like delusion, makes me feel very unsafe. You started out our conversation by asking my marital status. That felt pointed especially when you followed it up by saying you had no intention of marrying your fiancee. Later on in the conversation you let it be known that you had visited my exact area of London in 1997. You seemed to be letting me know that you knew where I lived.

I felt, therefore , it was imperative to use the clearest of terms to let you know that I had absolutely no intention of rekindling any form of relationship with you, nor of marrying anyone. I'm really not the marrying kind these days. I cannot express more clearly how I wish for closure for both of us.
The Diane you fell in love with is not me.

I'm sorry. Please forgive me. Thank you.

Diane

Part 5 Jezebel

Van 'The Man' & the Yellow Brick Road

I've just got back from walking the two family dogs. I'd put on my over-ear headphones and set out into the cold, drizzly winter weather. Normally, I would've really resisted this chore, especially in such dreary weather conditions, but music seemed like my ultimate hack to get anything done. As soon as music started playing in my ears, the rest of the world disappeared and I entered into this blissful place of connection. It was just me, the music and dare I say it, god?

Every song on my 'liked' songs shuffled playlist, seemed to be playing in a significant order to suit my present needs. I'd stepped out listening to the deeply spiritual and some might say, esoteric album Common One by Van Morrison.

It was not the usual upbeat music I normally listened to to get me up and going, but something deeply, spiritually connected, with lyrics that just seemed to hit the spot, being delivered as a message to me, right there, right then.

The Irish soul singer sang about giving up hope and being in despair, being on your own and taking a journey inside yourself with the help of angels to discover Source , the Oneness and ultimately never letting spirit die.

The music transported me back to my fifteen year old self, lying on my bed, the cassette tape player playing this album as loud as the speakers could handle. It would soothe me in ways I couldn't understand back then. I couldn't really understand the lyrics even though hearing them now, I realised they applied to my mental state back then. Van Morrison, in this particular album seemed to be able to hold me in a vibrational hug simply with the sound of his music and the intention of his lyrics. Now I know it was facilitating a connection to my higher self, to Source, to God.

He continued to sing about going inside on a journey and discovering a road, then following that road until it took you back home, walking step by step, one foot in front of the other, until you manage to turn things around.

At that time in my life, at 15, I had been cast as the Cowardly Lion in my new convent school's production of the Wizard of Oz. Following the yellow brick road to find your way home seemed to be a bit of a theme for me at the time. At 15, as the lion I was in search of my courage. Maybe this was the lion I was searching for on my adventures in Africa?

Maybe I didn't get to play Sally Bowles, but maybe having the opportunity to play the Lion in the Wizard of Oz was a more age appropriate way to explore my inner strength.

I was still living in fear of my mother uncovering my living a secret life. Her cage could not contain this wild beast that was the acting out of an unhealed child sexual abuse victim.

Every day, on my 15 minute walk to and from the convent school, I would carve out extra time by making up bogus after school activities, then I would do to strangers, what David had taught me to do to him.

37

Come Sit Here For A While, Little Diane

As Rizzo sang, in the movie, Grease, there were worse things I could do than get with a boy, or two.

Before I begin telling the story of this difficult chapter of my life, I want to sit quietly with my inner child of fifteen who others had named Jezebel. I'd gently take her hand and tell her that I'm here now and that she has nothing to be ashamed of. She is safe and protected and everything that happened to her was not her fault but the inevitable fallout of what happens to a child when their innocence is taken from them before their emotions are mature enough to cope.

I dedicate this part of the book to all children who carry shame into their adult lives because of something that happened to them at the hands of an adult who was meant to protect them, not harm them.

This is for you, and for you, Diane, my younger self.

38

Vampire at Christian Camp

I was perfectly set up to be the potential victim of a cult or a religious group looking for new members.

I'd joined a youth group, my mum said it would be good for me, and she felt safe with me going there. Christian Camp was a weekend away supervised youth camping adventure. I was very excited and happy to go. It started out great, I found myself fitting in, I was enjoying playing volleyball, loved the communal outdoor eating and everyone was super friendly. I actually felt normal here. This was unusual. I shared a small tent with two other girls, the boys had separate tents. The adults looking out for us were men in their early twenties, but they seemed super old to us.

The first night, I settled into my sleeping bag in the tent with the two girls, and we told ghost stories to one another as we messed around with shadows cast by our torches on the tent walls. Giggles and screeches rang out into the woodland camp site as we had our silly fun.

Then the tent flap suddenly unzipped and two pairs of hands grabbed my sleeping bag and pulled me, screaming, out of the tent. One of the assailants was a boy I recognised who had been flirting with me in the daytime, the other was one of the camp leaders. I fought them off with enough force and noise to make their attempt at kidnap far too obvious, so they slunk away into the darkness, leaving me a panicked mess on the muddy floor.

The next day we went swimming in the pool and that same boy from the night before jumped in next to me and started dunking me under the water. I panicked and bit him hard on the neck as I surfaced for air, before he dunked me yet again. This time I bit him so hard I drew blood, and the panic on his face made me realise that maybe I'd gone too far.

That evening, sitting around the campfire, the whole group teased me and laughed at me, calling me

'The Vampire.'

The boy I had bitten would strangely go on to write unwanted love letters to me until his unrequited attention just fizzled out. I was never interested in him anyhow. That moment of panic and biting was set into my subconscious brain and would emerge years later as a surprising response to any situation where I felt stuck or trapped.

I now recognise it as part of a meltdown behaviour.

39

Lion, meet Scarecrow

My sidekick in The Wizard of Oz was the Scarecrow, played by a young, fiery red- head called Cara.

When I first met her, I took an instant dislike to her. I didn't know why, she seemed perfectly pleasant.

Initially, I was drawn to the complex kids who felt exciting, but then I could never seem to make things work as a friendship.

I was a bit of a loner at the Convent, and no wonder, really. I had joined the school, right in the middle of the term, so I looked as if I'd been expelled or something equally dubious. Break times were spent indoors, reading in class.

The Irish Catholic nuns were brilliant. I know some people have not had such great experiences with nuns, but in my case I was blessed to have them look out for me. They decided I was a perfect candidate to be Cara's friend, who was, in her words, looking back at herself, deeply virginal.

Here I was, a Jezebel. Yin and Yang.

I think we were deliberately cast as Lion and Scarecrow, knowing it would force us to get to know one another.

It worked!

Cara and I bonded over a shared desire to buy a drum kit. We schemed and plotted, devising all sorts of ways of trying to make money. We settled eventually on making hand made necklaces from readily available shells on the beach across the road from the convent, stringing them on to leather strips.

The drum kit never materialised but the shared mission and focus created something far more valuable, a friendship that would last the test of time, a friendship for which I remain deeply grateful.

40

A Saved Jezebel

A few months later, I'd attend another church youth-group meeting and would be 'saved'.

Walking into the church hall, I could see a group of other young people already waiting for our arrival.

We all joined hands in a circle for fellowship and after a bit of prayer, people began to shake and speak in a sort of *'Shabala Habala'* way.

(I now know this is speaking in tongues, but at the time it felt very peculiar to witness first hand).

Then they'd fall to the floor and everyone would hug them and tell them that Jesus loved them.

I could feel my insides quivering again.

What was this funny feeling?

Now it was my turn to do the shaking and falling over thing.

Was I just copying to please? Trying to fit in?

If it really was the Holy Spirit or some form of power of suggestion, I'll never know, but I left that evening a saved young girl.

Lord knows, I needed saving. I knew I was a wicked, dirty, shameful girl. Maybe now I could start over?

Jan had also been saved, apparently. It had got back to me that people at his church were calling me a Jezebel and a demon.

Maybe I had been but not any longer!

So thank you, Jesus!

41

Makeovers and Confirmation Fraud

Our Lady Makeovers

During school holidays, the nuns would ask me to paint the outdoor statuary for them. This was the most fun job for a teenage girl with a developing sense of camp and kitsch. To be let loose with some paints to revamp Jesus with his bleeding sacred heart and Mary in her sweeping robes was so enjoyable.

Let's just say Mary looked far less modest and demure set among the greenery of the convent grounds, once I'd finished her makeover.

The nuns, though, appeared delighted with my efforts and would reward me by regifting me knickknacks that had been given to them previously by grateful parishioners. I treasured those kitsch porcelain vases and old lady ornaments.

Are you confirmed?

E ven though I was not Catholic (just a naughty girl) I would attend the weekly Mass as part of my convent education. The first one I ever attended was an experience I'll never forget.

My senses were dazzled as I entered the church. Dramatic, oftentimes gory representations of the various stations of the cross lined the walls, above them were the most fabulous colourful stained-glass windows depicting Christ and all the Angels and Saints. Large carved wooden statuary stood on the periphery, and the altar dazzled with its golden splendour. The rows of wooden pews creaked and gave off a musty sweet woody scent, and there was another enticing unfamiliar fragrance in the air that I later learned was frankincense. Once I'd gathered my widely scattered senses, I realised there was some sort of ritual I needed to follow before settling down on the benches. I copied the girl in front of me as she tapped her forehead, heart centre, then shoulders, left and right, then dipped down in a deep curtsey before filing into the pew. Then she kneeled on a cushion that she took off a peg hanging in front of the pew, placing it on the floor in front of her. I religiously copied her, keeping my eye on her as there was a lot of standing up, sitting down and kneeling to be done. Was this so that no-one fell asleep? There was also a call and response going on with the priest, "And also with you" was said over and over again. Bells rang out and the priest held up a goblet.

" This is the blood of Christ. "

More bells, more holding stuff up.

" The Body of Christ. "

I then followed my leader, queued up to get a wafer and a sip of wine from the priest out of the goblet. (Made me think of sexy farmer's loving cup).

The girl next to me whispered to me as we made our way back to our pew,

" Are you confirmed? "
" Confirmed for what? " I retorted.
She looked shocked.
" Are you even Catholic? "
I shook my head as she looked at me in absolute horror.

What? What had I done wrong now? Had she seen my Jezebel?

42

The Dowlings and Losing Jesus

The Dowlings

After the shaking, falling down, finding Jesus experience at the Youth Club, I was really keen to tell my friend Cara.

She would be so proud of me, as now we had Jesus in common.

Cara came from an Irish Catholic family. She had seven siblings, four brothers and three sisters. She was the baby of the family and lived in a large Emerald green house on the slopes of the mountainside overlooking the fishing harbour in Kalk Bay.

The family matriarch, Eve, was a wonderful woman. To this day, I credit her with being my first true feminist role model. She was outwardly stern and came across at first as a little haughty, but once you got to know her, you quickly learned of her deep and generous kind heart. She spoke with a perfect received English accent reminiscent of early BBC broadcasting tonality, no trace of any South African twang at all, which just added to her special aura and commanding presence. Eve was a broadcaster, actor and Estate Agent, an independent woman who had single-handedly brought up her family after the early death of her husband, and she had done it brilliantly.

The family were warm, creative, open- minded, all unique characters, all bonded together with great love for their mother. This family would end up being my chosen family for a significant part of my early life.

Finding then losing Jesus

After I got home from being saved, I picked up my guitar and started singing songs about Jesus.

I felt giddy and excited, proud not to be Jezebel any longer. I dug out a dusty copy of the Bible from my parents' bookshelf and started reading passages from its yellowed pages out loud.

Not able to hold it in any longer, I had to share this good news with Cara.

I picked up the telephone and dialled her number. As soon as she picked up the receiver, I shouted down the phone,

" Cara, you'll never guess what? I've found Jesus! "

Her lack of response was surprising, throwing me off guard.

" Oh. Where did you find him? "

A typical dry humour comment from her.

" Aren't you excited for me? I'm going to be baptised on Muizenberg beach tomorrow. I've got to wear a white dress, I can't wait! "

Cara's response was polite. I wouldn't understand her reaction until I was much older.

I did go to the beach the next day, but no-one turned up.

Had I got the date wrong? Perhaps. It was a miraculous intervention either way.

Jesus fizzled out for me after that. I'm sure that Cara was relieved.

43

Craig

The years between fourteen and nineteen are challenging to recall, but I'll endeavour to claw back whatever memories I have.

It was a time of contrasts, some people tried to look after me and love me, while others were taking advantage of my acting out and autistic naivety. Typically, I couldn't tell the difference, even though these two intentions were complete polar opposites.

After Jan had been cut out of the picture and David had disappeared into oblivion, (I found out years later that David had written letters to me that my mother had secretly intercepted and disposed of) my attention was swayed by a young man with long blonde hair who had just moved into the small house directly opposite ours. From our living room window, his front door was clearly visible. There was a large tree directly in front of his house, and I'd spotted him standing, peeking at me from behind it. Then one afternoon, as I looked at him through the window, he gestured to the tree, then went back inside his house. I made an excuse, and ran across the road to the tree, to find a small note folded up tightly and wedged into the rough bark of the tree. It said simply,

" Hello neighbour, my name is Craig. "

That was the start of another note passing adventure.

I soon caught considerable feelings for this mysterious, shy surfer dude. My heart would skip a beat every time I heard his Volkswagen camper van chug up the steep hill that was our shared road. I would instantly lose my appetite mid-meal, as my stomach would lurch and seem to find its way up into my throat when I knew he'd just returned home.

What is that crazy chemistry of teenage crushes? The memories of these heady feelings are still so tangible all these years later. We would eventually both pluck up the courage to meet when my parents were conveniently out of the way, and he would take me driving in his van and introduce me to JJ Cale and Bruce Springsteen. I can't listen to JJ Cale's Hey Baby without those heady feelings coming rushing back to me through time and space.

Despite his ways of connecting with me being similar to those of David's, actually he couldn't have been more different. Craig seemed very aware upon meeting me of the age-gap and physically kept his distance, which confused my fifteen-year-old self. Didn't he like me? Maybe I wasn't pretty enough? He knew I had a crush on him and would let me loose in his house whilst he went surfing. That felt special.

Looking back now from my adult perspective, I can still see that our interaction was probably still inappropriate, but ultimately, Craig has always felt like one of the good guys.

44

I've Been Told That You've Been Bold

Andrew and Paul

I can't remember how it came about, but I ended up with another boyfriend
, Andrew. I can't work out where I met him, as by this stage I was at an all-girls convent. Even more befuddling was the fact that my mum allowed me to have a boyfriend after the Jan disaster at all.

But here we were.

All I remember of this young man was that I always felt insecure about his feelings towards me. He spoke constantly of his ex, which was confusing to me.

I ended up being caught in a compromising situation with him by my mother just before things were about to get heated between us. I remember Mum getting proper angry and telling me to keep my door open at all times.

Later I remember because it was such a rare thing, completely losing my temper with my mother and shouting at her so loudly that I lost my voice for the day. Looking back, that was probably a meltdown, as I was far too afraid to dare risk raising my voice to her normally.

It confused me that Mum had let boys back into the picture once more. Why hadn't she ever had the conversation with me about why I had been sexually active at fourteen in the first place? She must've thought it was all coming from Jan. But then the letters from David that she intercepted must've given her some sort of clue as to what had happened? Maybe she was just in deep denial? Where were her warning bells? Was my behaviour normal to her because she too had gone through similar experiences? I can only speculate.

I was allowed to invite my boyfriend to a New Year's Eve party held at my house when I was around 16. That is when I met Paul. He kissed me at midnight and sparks flew. By this time, it had become clear that Andrew wasn't really interested in me as his girlfriend.

Now I look back and wonder if he had heard anything about me on the grapevine and was there to see what he could get, not much while my mum was around. Again, this is speculation, but it seems to fit the pattern.

Paul became the perfect boyfriend for me in my mother's eyes. He was attentive to her, polite and generous, buying her flowers and expensive whiskey. He was in the Air Force, had a car and was a decent chap. However, when Mum was in the living room, Paul and I would be engaging in rather risky but thrilling behaviour in the kitchen, right under my mother's nose. How we didn't get caught, I'll never know.

From my perspective, I was treated with nothing but kindness, respect, and love by Paul. We had wonderful times together while it lasted. Then, like all South African young men, he had to go off to a camp, he was duty bound to serve a short stint of military service. While he was away, he'd asked his very camp and quirky friend Michael to look out for me.

Michael wrote surreal short stories and had the best sense of humour, and I thoroughly enjoyed his company. I didn't find him the least bit attractive. I wouldn't let that minor detail get in the way of going through the motions of doing to him what I'd done with all the other boys. At the time, I remember feeling discombobulated by my behaviour because he didn't particularly want what I was offering, nor did I feel sexually attracted to him. Here I was, yet again, forcing my pleasing self rather awkwardly on this very startled, most probably autistic, potentially gay young man.
I knew it was wrong, yet I couldn't stop.

Now I look back and can see how the cycle of the abused becoming the abuser can happen. Right there, I had myself become an abuser.
Paul would later find out and quite rightly break up with me.
I felt ashamed, embarrassed, and confused.
I started sneaking alcohol out of my parent's drink cabinet.
After this time, things started spiralling horribly out of control.

Knocking and Tomasz

Random boys who I'd never met before started turning up on my doorstep asking for me by name. The word had clearly got around and things felt really unsafe. I was running out of excuses to explain away these incidences to my parents. I had no idea how this had all come about. The next man I was involved with was a Polish man called Tomasz. I'd met him through a friend of a friend. He'd come and take me out in his camper van and when my parents weren't home, he'd come in my house, and we'd have sex on my mother's bed.

I know, I know.

One particular incident sticks in my memory. Tomasz had come to visit, and he had come up the stairs leading up to the front door and had touched me on my waist. My whole body went into fight or flight mode and I ran down the stairs, pushing past him and into the road, running as fast as I could to get away, while he stood there looking puzzled. Eventually, I calmed down, and I came back with no idea why my body had reacted in such a way.

Mama don't like no guitar playing round here.

I'd taken to playing my guitar on the front porch when I wasn't sneaking around with boys. I'd play and sing songs by Leonard Cohen, not very well, mind, but I tried my best. Ever since I'd borrowed Songs of Love and Hate on Vinyl from the local library quite by chance, I'd become quite obsessed with the dark tortured soul of this poet who played such beautiful guitar. I didn't quite know what he was saying in the lyrics, but my heart connected with the essence of the music, and it soothed my soul.

All through this time, I was a star pupil at the convent. I excelled in many subjects. The nuns loved me, so much so that on prize giving night, I came away with trophies for creative writing and mathematics and a book prize for general knowledge of world affairs. This prize puzzled me, as I knew nothing of the matter. I think the nuns made it up because they just liked me or something. I wonder if they'd have still liked me if they knew what I was doing out of school hours.

My Jezebel was in full self-harming mode at this point, using random penis like other girls used blades to slice and bleed. Things would come to a head on one day a few months later when I would be told to pack my bags and leave.

The little old lady neighbours, who I would help carry shopping up and down the steep hill of our road, had been listening to my guitar playing. They'd also been watching the comings and goings at my house while my parents were working, apparently, and thought it was a good idea to report this information back to my mother.

Because my mum couldn't save face from this very public humiliation, there was no other option for her but to ask me to leave. So at 16 going on 17, I moved into the Emerald Greenhouse, the family home of my dear Scarecrow friend, Cara. I was welcomed in to their home like the prodigal daughter and became another rescued soul.

45

Out of the Frying Pan into the Fire

Bluto, and a Good Kicking

I started frequenting the local pub, The Brass Bell. It wasn't a regular pub, but a bar/restaurant that perched between the railway station and the sea. The outdoor seating area was directly next to the breaking waves. It was a very exciting place to be, especially on a weekend when I would go to the live jazz sessions and outdoor fish braai. I looked old enough to drink (even though I wasn't quite) and drinks were bought for me by men who were trying to get to know me.

One of these people was a dark man in his early 30s with piercing blue eyes and dark facial hair. He intrigued me. I would start to see him on a fairly regular basis, but at his home a short drive away. I noticed evidence of a woman's presence in his home: a frilly house-coat hanging behind the bathroom door and perfume bottles. This led me to wondering if he was married. While I was there one afternoon, there was a knock on his door and I panicked, perhaps that was his wife? It was his next door neighbour, a blonde man of a similar age. The dark man, whose name I cannot recall, but I'll call him Ian, asked did I mind if his friend joined in? I had no idea how to say no, advocating for my own needs was a skill I hadn't been able to master and by this point I presumed my body was for others' pleasure, so I just nodded meekly.

Later, another man would join and sit in the corner in a chair, staring at the goings-on.

The next time Ian took me to his flat, he said he wanted to introduce me to someone. So we got into his car and drove a short while down the road. He pulled up outside a block of flats. We climbed a few flights of stairs and knocked on a door. After a few moments, the door opened, and I saw a man who I can only describe as looking like Bluto from Popeye, very fat with large, bulging eyes and a black beard. I recoiled in fear, Ian shoved me in the small of my back, pushing me into this ogre's lair.

Bluto gestured to a bed, he flopped down into a chair at the foot of the bed, facing it and barked out at me, "Masturbate!"

So, with no other option than to comply, I did, and I put on a performance any porn actor would be proud of, it felt like my life depended on it.

All the time, I was reassuring myself that at least he hadn't touched me.

Afterwards Bluto grunted his approval, exchanged something with Ian(I never saw exactly what) and Ian drove me home in silence.

I refused to see Ian after that experience.

However, the third wheel man who would sit in the corner of the room observing, during visits to Ian's home, turned up one Saturday evening at the Brass Bell, during a disco session outside. I was in my element dancing solo, which really suited me. A scattering of people were sat drinking at tables outside, chatting and facing the waves. No-one seemed to notice as this man grabbed me, dragged me to the ground and started punching and kicking me as I lay helpless in shock. He kept saying I was a bitch for not letting him have his turn.

No-one saw, no-one helped. It was like no-one cared. Was he even there, or was this just my demons torturing me? Clearly I deserved it.

Eight Men and a Suitcase.

I'm just going to write this fast so I can get it over with. Don't know the date or the context of how I got there in the first place, but here's a memory of when I was around 17.

I was casually seeing a man called Reg, he was well known in the community. He ran a successful seafood restaurant, he was a cool, entrepreneur, blonde, surfer dude type. I was very flattered he'd want to spend time with me, after all, I was still at school and he was a proper success story. He lived in a beautiful home that was set on a Marina, the estuary was just on the other side of his patio doors and the sunsets over the water in the evenings were breathtakingly spectacular, romantic, dare I say?

One evening, we'd come back to his, and we'd settled in for a snuggle in his bed when there was a loud knock on the door. He answered it and eight white men pushed their way in.

Reg looked scared and panicked. They were all shouting, "Where's the stuff?"

They pushed past Reg roughly, and came into the bedroom.

One of the men saw me cowering naked under the sheet and called the others in to come and have a look.

One of them walked over to the wardrobe, looking for something. He seemed to find what they'd come looking for as he brought down from the top of the wardrobe, a large suitcase.

"Got it!" he shouted.

The rest of the group, including Reg, all rushed in to the bedroom.

Reg tried to grab the suitcase, but it was a futile endeavour with eight against one. He had no chance of retrieving this valuable case. He looked perturbed and angry. The man holding the suitcase teasingly above Reg's head said,

"I tell you what, Reg, you can have this (the case) if we can have that"(pointing at me, hiding under the sheet).

So it was that I was gang raped by all eight men in exchange for whatever there was in that suitcase.

One of the men I recognised, he was a local and I knew he was getting married the following day.

Was I deliberately marking a man in a place that his future bride would see the next day, hoping she'd ask him awkward questions? Or was it a trauma response that began at that Christian camp? It didn't much matter at that moment. I sank my teeth deep into his neck as he was at his most distracted at the peak of his pleasure. He howled, grasped his neck and shouted,

"Watch out! This bitch bites!"

"Explain that to your wife tomorrow" I hissed as he climbed off me and the next man in the queue climbed on.

Years later, in an act of reclaiming my power, I would organise myself an eight-man gang bang with a group of married men who did this sort of thing for fun. I don't know whether this was a wise thing to do, (I certainly wouldn't recommend it) but at the time it felt right.

Most men who embarked on this lifestyle were married. They explained this away by saying what the wife doesn't know, won't hurt her. (Another nail in the marriage coffin for me.) They also said there were fewer risks of sexually transmitted diseases if the men involved were married. I wasn't sure about the logic there, to be fair, although I certainly made sure they all used condoms and practiced safe sex.

We had our consensual fun and afterwards, as they were hanging around having their post-coital cigarette, one of the men rather stupidly asked me why I'd organised this event. I think he was expecting some sort of small talk, like "I'm a freak," answer that would bolster his ego and his world view on women's sexuality.

Let me just say here that one should be careful asking an autistic person a question you would rather not hear the truth from.

"I was raped by eight men, this was my way of neutralising that event. I can't really explain how it worked, but it did."

The man was appalled and clearly outraged with this answer. He told me he felt used and exploited. I had felt no guilt in this situation. Really, dude? A mere ten minutes previously, he looked like he was having the most fun. Which one was it, and what about his wife?

46

The Green House & The Wild Bird

Bird sketch found in Imogen's journal

Just the other day, during a very intense bodywork session with my dear friend Sakli, I had a massive revelation. Paradoxically, my Jezebel was trying to keep me safe by putting me in risky situations.

She was also making me write it down in a journal, making it more likely I'd be discovered.

The reason being, anyone and anywhere felt safer than my unpredictable mother, who had violently screamed at me and manipulated me into telling her who I preferred as my parent. Jezebel was acting out, ensuring I'd be caught and be thrown out.

During my session, my inner child, little Diane, sobbed and muttered quietly,

"I'm scared of you, mummy,"

over and over, and she finally surrendered the sobs with a whispered admission,

"but I still love you".

I realised that after the core wound of my mother screaming "You bitch!" at me after finding out the truth that I hadn't chosen her, I had put myself in a situation where I felt that at any moment she would wreak revenge on me for hurting her pride so deeply.

I realise now from my mother's extreme behaviours throughout my life that I was dealing with a grandiose narcissist who I had humiliated by telling her my truth: that I didn't like her and I preferred my dad. Once you provoke narcissistic rage, there is always a price to be paid for deciding not to feed them any more. How very dare you deny them their source of supply! As an only child until the age of fourteen, I had been her primary source of supply, now clearly I had declared war on her and gone into competition with her for her secondary fuel source, the male gaze!

I would go on to describe this narcissistic mother envy of the teenage daughter as Snow-White syndrome.

Around this chaotic time, my mother gave birth to my half-sister.

I never really had the chance to get to know her properly as by the time she was three, I had been told to pack my bags and get out. As traumatic as this moment should've been (I thought it would've been seared into my memory), I must confess that I've had trouble recalling the details of this time. Maybe the feeling I felt ultimately was that of relief? Finally, Jezebel had done it, she had got me out of there. I felt relief at the news of my mother's death around twenty years later, so this rings true.

Just like Dorothy in Munchkinland, I set off with my basket (alas not with Toto) down the yellow brick road, well around the corner and up the mountainside, a mere ten-minute walk and I arrived at my own personal version of Emerald City: the Green house, the home of my scarecrow friend, Cara, and her family.

I was taken in with open, loving arms, welcomed like the prodigal lost daughter.

(I later found out that I wasn't the first to be taken in like this, and I wouldn't be the last, such was the generous spirit and kind-heartedness of this family unit).

Where my home life was tense and uptight, life at the Green House was chaotic yet relaxed, cosy and comforting.

At home, there would be weekly budget meetings around the kitchen table, where I was expected to account for every last cent spent of my meagre pocket money. I would plot and scheme and collude with my mum's domestic help, (the maid) how we'd get revenge on my mum who treated her so badly and disrespectfully. The weekends would be lost to tidying and cleaning, and after school times taken up with my preparing dinner before my mother came back from work.

Life at the Green House was a refreshing change. Everything stopped at 4pm for tea. One of the four sisters, often Biddy, would bring out home baked goods and a big porcelain teapot filled with fragrant Earl Grey tea. Everyone present in the house at the time would join in with this comforting, homely ritual. For the first time in my life, I felt accepted for exactly who I was. No longer walking on eggshells, I could feel my entire nervous system relax, and my body breathe out in a big sigh of relief.

Creativity ran through the Green house like its lifeblood. Nuala, Cara's youngest sister, would go on to become a poet and established author. I remember being awed by her big brown doe eyes and shiny bouncy curls and her being so immersed in drawing and writing in her room. Tessa, another of the sisters, was a free-spirited performer and languages creative. We would both indulge in staging in house cabaret style performances. Her infamous act being a striptease where she'd start off with many layers of clothing, the gag being that she'd never be able to reach the denouement because there was always another layer of clothing to go. I would channel my inner drag queen, though I'd sing rather than lip-synch, belting out camp classics like Big Spender from Sweet Charity, Cabaret, (obviously) and the Wild Bird song, the first aria from Carmen. I was in my element, my creative beast had been let out of its cage and fed.

Translation of the lyrics from French into English of this aria, that I would sing repeatedly, revealed that I had been singing about myself all along.

L'amour est un oiseau rebel.

Love is a wild bird that no-one can tame
And you waste your time trying to catch it.
Nothing helps, not threats, nor pleas,
You may talk to me passionately, yet I'll pick a man who never says a word,
That's love, that's love, that's love,
Love is a gypsy child who never follows the rules,
If you don't love me, I still might love you
And if I love you
Watch out.

Just writing out these lyrics brings tears of connection to my eyes as I think of my inner gypsy wild bird child, longing to stretch her wings and fly. That final warning of watch out , I knew I'd directed at my mother.

Begrudgingly, Jezebel still loved her.

47

You Shall Go to the Ball

After about a year of living at the Green House, my mum would reach back out and ask me to come home. I have no idea what prompted this change of heart. I can only guess that my stepdad, Hennie, had something to do with it.

By this point, I had left school with a glowing final report with academic results that would have made any parent proud. I can only send little Diane a big well done for managing to rise above such disruption and chaos and still come out of her education unscathed.

I reluctantly left the sanctuary of the Green House and moved back into my old room and set about trying to work out my next steps in life. Potentially, the world was my oyster. I had always been a Jack of all trades, doing well wherever I placed my focus. Deep down, I knew what I really wanted to do, but I knew it was completely out of the question because mum had always said that I wasn't good enough to be able to succeed at it. That forbidden, taboo thing was art.

Art, where I found my joy, expression and solace, escaping into line, form, texture and colour, getting lost in subconscious doodling that people would remark upon. This would surprise me as, obviously, I was a rubbish artist. Where had I formed this belief? When I was around ten years old, my mother came into my bedroom and sat next to me, quietly watching me draw.

I was copying an image from a magazine that had taken my fancy, relishing the challenge of finding just the right type of descriptive line to define the form and make my drawing as accurate as possible. For me, copying photographs was as satisfying to my brain as doing a complicated jigsaw puzzle, searching for that perfect gestural line to finish the picture. Mum quietly observed me draw and then said the words that would take root and grow into a toxic stranglehold of inhibition in my consciousness.

"You'll never be an artist, you can only copy. Real artists draw from their imaginations."

That moment marks the exact timestamp that shut me down but would ultimately be the piece of gritty resistance to my creative pearl, that would drive me forward ultimately to prove her words wrong.

Who knows what lay behind my mother's repeated attempts at shutting down my creativity?

First, it was this poisonous earworm that would echo around my subconscious each time my creative urges would push up to the surface. Then it was my mother's insistence that I was to be the only child in the entire school not to be taught (compulsory subject) art. It felt as if Mum saw art as something that would seduce me, rather like boys, and lead me to a life of... what? Decadence? Struggle? I could possibly understand the motivation of a parent to steer their child away from a life of guaranteed penury. Especially given the widely touted cliché of the starving artist in his garret, but at what price is happiness and following your path? It amuses me now to know I live a stone's throw away from where starving artist Vincent van Gogh lived when staying in London. He didn't earn a single penny from his work when living, if it hadn't had been for his brother supporting him financially, he wouldn't have created the incredible art legacy that he has left behind. It is tough to make it as an artist, even a great artist, so maybe Mum had valid fears?

My other theory is that Mum had her own artistic talents that she didn't allow herself to indulge in. Seeing me find joy in art reminded her of what she was denying herself. The only clue to this theory was the one time she told me she would paint watercolours of fairies, then when her dad died, she just stopped.

This seems to ring true as in her later years, I would encourage her to explore her creative side, by starting back up drawing and painting. She would email me to say she'd bought all the materials but lacked the confidence to make any sort of mark. For this, I can find compassion in her actions towards me as a child. Witnessing my freedom in creativity made her even more acutely aware of her self-imposed prison.

When it came to deciding what my next educational steps would be, Mum was clear: I was to study computing at university because I had a logical brain, was good at maths and computers were the future. I could see the reasoning behind this plan, but my heart didn't respond to this suggestion at all. I knew Mum had just started a new job implementing computer systems at the workplace, so it was an obvious choice for me in her eyes. It was when my stepdad quietly suggested that art school could be an interesting option for me since I was so good at drawing.

My soul leaped in excitement. YES! YES!

But can I? Am I allowed? Is this even an option? Is this even a career path?

Hennie assured me that he'd speak to my mum, and they'd come up with a plan together.

The plan was that I was to attend the technical college that offered work placements immediately on graduation, and I would study graphic design, as all college leavers left with job offers on that course. It seemed like the perfect compromise. I'd be doing art and getting a job. I'd also be moving into my own shared student flat with one of my classmates.

At last, I was leaving home!

Mum and Hennie agreed they were happy to pay my college fees and part rental if I picked up a part-time job to cover the balance. I interviewed successfully for a Saturday job in an art supplies and picture framing shop and got a lunchtime waitressing shift in a restaurant just up the road from college.

This bird was finally going to stretch out her wings!

It would soon become very apparent that graphic design was not the right fit for this chaotic baby creative. I repeatedly failed my lettering assignments but was consoled by my tutors that because my life drawing skills were so strong, that a transfer to the fine art department would be a far better fit for me. So it was that I had managed to break free and started out on my path to becoming a real artist.

Mum had not finished yet.

She would soon pull the rug out from under my feet yet again.

The first day of walking into art school will always remain in my memory. I had painted up a pair of plain white plimsols for the occasion, an image of my bare feet was painted on the tops of my shoes. I think this memory fixed itself in my memory bank because I must have spent an awful lot of time awkwardly staring down at my feet.

Such was the overwhelming anticipation of a whole new social environment to get used to. An entirely new bunch of humans to get to know, terrifying and exciting in equal measures.

We were first all led into the big drawing studio to be introduced to the staff. I was surprised and delighted to see the familiar face of my Cape Town High art teacher, Mr Stander, among their throng. I felt comforted by his familiar face and breathed out a little. I still felt ridiculously nervous, but I fixed my gaze on my silly plimsols and listened.

"Hands up if you did art at school"

Most of the group put up their hands.

"Those of you who didn't raise your hand, congratulations, you have a head start as we won't have to undo everything they teach you in school".

The staff all giggled knowingly at their shared jest.

That was interesting, mum trying to stop me from doing art at school had actually given me an advantage here.

After the welcome talk, we were all thrown straight into the deep end, heading into a life drawing session with two nude models. I could hear the inevitable embarrassed sniggers from some new intake, but I was ready and serious.

From that moment on, I discovered just how much I loved drawing the human form and how exquisitely difficult it was to capture life and sustain deep concentration. I could see obviously in my drawings where I had been tuned in and at one with the model. A section of the elbow, for example, would re- ally feel tense and bony, the quality of the line would clearly communicate the form from 3D to 2D. Then as my eyes journeyed along the form, I would see how my mind had wandered, distraction won out, and I would see how clumsy and flabby the line became. To me, life drawing was the ultimate challenge. I could read my at tempts to capture form like I was reading music: here it was sharp, here it was flat and here completely out of tune. I wanted not only to capture the form of the sitter, but also the energy, the mood, the movement, and spirit. What an incredible challenge lay before me!

I was at once fired up and then, after a moment of trying and failing to live up to the standards of my inner challenge, completely overwhelmed. Art introduced me to the inner workings of my brain and my huge and impressive capacity to self sabotage through the pursuit of perfection. These two years of art school would introduce me to the 'zone' where I would lose time immersed in painting and reawaken, shaking and exhilarated having speedily completed a painting in a frenzied, trance like state. It took me a while to be able to access this.

Initially, I struggled trying to find my subject. I knew I wasn't an abstract painter. My creative practice would involve people in one form or another because people fascinate me. I started out painting clumsy, awkward, illustrative paintings of people based on photographs, with brushes and oil paint on canvas because I thought that was how it was done. Just like in so many areas of my life, my choices were bound up in some strange preconceptions of normal. Techniques were not taught in this department, instead we were encouraged to discover through application and play, things that worked for us. Emphasis was placed on individual expression and finding of ones own voice. There was one slight problem, I had no idea what my voice was, and my early paintings reflected this. When a visiting lecturer looked at one of my paintings and suggested that I try something radically different.

"Try painting with your fingers," he said, at the start, I thought he was joking.

I gave it a go regardless. I changed from painting on bouncy rough canvas, with brushes, to using my fingers and palms on smooth board. This seemingly silly suggestion unlocked something inside of me.

Soon I would become that student observed walking around campus, board under one arm, bag of oil paints and rags, in the other, searching for a willing victim, ready to sit for a portrait for half an hour. After this short time, I would be faced with a completed portrait that would be wild and expressive, painted in a flurry of oil paint finger dabs and swooshes. It was like I had ten brushes available to me at one go. My fingers could now keep up with the speed that my brain/eye connection required.

This is not a recommended practice, however. Oil paint can be highly toxic and is easily absorbed through the skin. Back then, ignorance was bliss.

This was a period of my life where I felt the most liberated and fulfilled. Jezebel had been mostly vanquished. I lived and breathed art. Some of my fellow students were totally inspirational, making my art school days exciting times to live through.

There was Rory, who today is a professional artist residing in Sweden, who I already knew as a colourful local in Kalk Bay, (his parties were legendary, fancy dress of course, the more surreal the better. The most memorable, was the night he dressed up as a Gratis Monster (Afrikaans for a Free Sample) a delightful play on words and performance. Rory's art is light-hearted, colourful, and surreal, with a nod to the shadows of life. I loved it back then and still love it today.

His depiction of large, voluptuous naked women with decorative and inviting vulvas, silly men with ridiculous erect out of control penises and dogs, so many dogs, so many of them in the humiliating shitting pose. How he squeezed so much joy from the profane and the ugly, I'll never know, but he remains one of my favourite artists to this day. The one time we hooked up, joyfully, he told me I had a beautiful body. I'll never forget his kind, artistic gaze, and afterwards he ate a tin of smoked oysters and drank the oil from the tin with a decadent, sexy flourish. Thank you, Rory, you showed me a whole new way of being. He also warned me against ever getting married when he told me he was getting married. (I'll never forget the row of sobbing women at his wedding ceremony. It was straight out of a telly novella) That warning confused me at the time, not any longer. Marriage certainly is not for me. Maybe he saw that in me back then. One of Rory's finest and most memorable moments at art college was shaving all of his hair, including eyebrows, and running through the streets naked.

Or was that just an urban legend? Rory, you'll have to let me know.

The other human who deeply affected me during these times was a mature student named Vacek. He was a gay, Czech national professional ice skater who had defected to South Africa from communist Czechoslovakia during a global ice skating tour. He was a wiry, bearded handsome man with twinkling kind eyes and I took to him immediately. His work was mainly screen prints and body mono prints, sometimes abstract, most times risqué. I loved him. He looked out for me when I was burning the candle at both ends during my time involved with Sam, the bar man. I was operating on very little sleep, dashing off on lunch break to work the waitressing shift, then back to college to finish my work there. He picked up on my vulnerability and would invite me to his home for dinner and a film, and would fuss over me like the mother I always wished I could have. He showed me such love and kindness during these times that I get quite emotional recalling those times spent together. Thank you, Vacek.

The most exciting thing I ever experienced in life happened at art college.

A visiting lecturer brought his concept of art marathons to South Africa. His concept was based on the theory that true creativity is accessed when the mind gives up trying to control. His way of getting the mind to surrender was by exhausting it. This was done through stimulating it with loud classical music, depriving it of knowledge of the passing of time, (blocking out natural light and using bright artificial lighting to create dramatic shadows on the models) and by pushing through the natural self consciousness that happens initially between model and artist. Once this barrier was broken, allowing the artist to truly look and the model to be truly seen, magic would happen. I can't even begin to use words to describe what went on in that eighteen-hour session. (Models were on a rota system, in case you were wondering) but by the end of it, I was in a different dimension. It felt transcendent, psychedelic even. I was producing the most beautiful pieces of art I had ever attempted, so effortlessly. Of course, it was exhausting, but we were young and resilient.

The music of Sade, John Cooper Clark, Klaus Nomi, Rodriguez and the political dub poems of Brixton resident Linton Kwesi Johnson were the soundtracks to my paintings. I had no idea I would go on to make Brixton my home, and would walk past the poet himself in the high street, quite unable to express my excitement at seeing such an inspiration in the flesh. Music and painting seem to seamlessly blend to create a sensory other-world, an escape into a future place, a place where the world was kinder, more beautiful, more accommodating of difference.

It's 2025, and I've just watched Elon Musk, the South African billionaire oligarch techbro racist, blatantly do two Nazi salutes at President Trump's inauguration. Maybe things just have to get far worse, so there is no coming back to this place, before they can change? The world out there frustrates and annoys me, but I refuse to be afraid. I will keep on creating and dreaming up a better place for all of us gorgeous freaks to coexist in harmony, acknowledging our differences and appreciating our similarities.

48

Jesus Wants YOU!

During these art school times, Jesus would make a final attempt to be in my life.

Actually, that's not accurate, people misrepresenting him in a bid to make money from a cult, fronted by the appearance of Christianity, would attempt to save me once more.

Obviously, it seemed as if I had a big sticker saying Jezebel on my forehead, I was quite the target. Clearly, Jesus's last attempt at washing away my sins hadn't worked.

Let me set the scene:

I was nineteen and flat sharing with another art student called Monique. She was a wild, free-spirited, Bohemian, dark-haired girl with bright blue eyes and a huge artistic talent. Her parents were Dutch and really kind, having invited me to their home for dinner to get to know the girl living with their daughter. I admired Monique so much, and enjoyed being her flatmate. She was fond of incense, the devil's lettuce and possessed the most exquisite lyrical style of drawing. We got on well right from the start, she turned a blind eye to my occasional evening visitors and had a few of her own. It was a fun time to be young, creative and exploring life together on our terms.

We started out so well, even coming up with our peculiar version of a pet: a random collection of hand sewn body parts that we added to and moved around the flat, a sort of soft sculpture, I suppose. We shared similar values and dreams, had a similar outlook on life, art, and everything. Things were going swimmingly, and then everything changed when Monique found Jesus.

Overnight, she gave up all of her vices. Some may say that included any sense of fun.

Tragically, she considered drawing to be one of her vices.

She told me that the Lord had gifted her a new talent to replace the sinful drawing of naked people, and that was the gift of song. There was only one problem I could see with that, Monique was tone-deaf. This makes for an amusing story, but the reality of living with someone constantly reading out loud from the Bible and singing worship songs excruciatingly out of tune was unbearable. I'm now aware that one of my biggest sensory triggers is sound. Sudden loud noise and music that is out of tune can easily tip me over into full meltdown. I cannot bear to be in a room where somebody performing music is just above or below the note, it's like nails down a chalkboard in discomfort levels for me. The outcome of weeks of this audible torture, resulted in my visiting the doctor, who diagnosed me with stress induced gastritis. I was given medication for the pain in my stomach and told to chill out. Bar Monique moving out or falling out of favour with Jesus, that was unlikely. She continued to burst into my room, feverishly preaching at me from the Bible at random times of day and night. She begged me to attend her church meetings. I would finally relent, just to stop the torture of the constant pleading. (This would be a pattern that would show up later on in my life, much to my detriment.)

The impact on my well-being fades in comparison to how this 'conversion' was affecting Monique's life. It was like her brain had been taken over by a parasite and Monique's body was its host.

I've no idea what her lovely parents must have thought about her dropping out of art school to follow this church.

I reluctantly agreed to join Monique at one of her outdoor church meetings after being worn down by her sheer persistence. Maybe once I saw what was going on, I'd be able to help her return to herself?

We set off early in the morning to the northern flank of Table Mountain, at the base of the land mass known as Devil's Peak. We were meeting the church group at Rhodes Memorial, an outdoor monument consisting of a small temple like structure with Doric columns, built of granite, housing a bust of the coloniser, diamond mogul and slave trader, Cecil John Rhodes. In front of this temple structure is a staircase made up of 49 broad steps, cut into the mountainside, one for each of Rhode's life, flanked either side by eight stone lions who look out over Cape Town below. It forms a natural and impressive amphitheatre that many groups back then (including Satanists at the dead of night) would utilise as a free outdoor venue and meeting place. Today it was this Christian group's turn to gather. I had dressed head to toe in black, and I stood in stark contrast to the rest of the group, who were dressed in white or high key colours. I just wished it over before it began as I'd only agreed to be there to appease Monique and hopefully put an end to her attempting to recruit me.

The morning went a little like this: Upbeat Christian songs were blasted out from speakers to whip up the energy, while this was happening I spotted people standing on the periphery who seemed to be directing the proceedings. They would nod and signal subtly to one another to bring the energy down at a certain point and slide into a slow, emotional prayer-like hymn.

My natural pattern seeking brain watched cynically as I observed the meticulously stage-directed performance of a spiritual experience, designed to create something (at this stage I wasn't sure what). I kept taking mental notes. After the atmosphere was set, a preacher was invited to the front to do his 'thing' and his thing apparently was conversions, bringing new followers to Jesus. He started out quietly, saying Jesus had told him that there were people ready to serve him, and they were to come to the front of the congregation to receive the POWER of Christ. (emphasis placed so you can hear how he spoke.)

Several people got up and filed forward, doing the falling over, *habala shabala* thing after the preacher pushed them on the forehead.

I was not amused by this. Once bitten, twice cynical.

I noticed that the preacher seemed to be looking straight at me as he said,

"Jesus is telling me it's a girl."

Was I being paranoid? Then I realised I was all in black, so I thought it was just an obvious place to rest his eyes on, looking over the congregation. He continued,

"Yes! A girl, he's calling this girl to receive his blessings."

My brain started to whirr. Was this whole thing for my benefit? Were they targeting me? Had Monique set me up? Surely not.

I sat and watched even closer, observing all the minute details of the people around me as this performance continued. The preacher seemed to be growing in frustration as more people, this time only women and girls, filed forward, eager to receive Jesus' blessing. I was struck by the preacher's growing agitation. This felt counter-intuitive. Why wasn't he celebrating his extraordinary conversion rate, evidenced all around him as people lay on the ground writhing and sobbing in religious ecstasy?

He continued,

"The Lord is telling me that there is someone who needs healing in the stomach region, Jesus invites you to be healed by his glory, step forward!"

Now that felt suspiciously specific.

I looked around to see the men who had been stage directing with gestures, all staring directly at me. I thought the preacher was going to blow a fuse, and we'd all witness some sort of holy human spontaneous combustion imminently. The preacher stared straight at me in frustration as I sat, a lone girl in a black dress, on the cold granite steps.

"IT'S YOU!!"
He pointed directly at me, unable to contain his frustration any longer.

Me? Inside, I battled with the inner urge to please and placate, and I pictured this as a holy war between the devil and an angel. Clearly I was the devil. This time the devil won out. I sat there and shook my head. The preacher gestured to the henchmen stage directors who then gave a signal to a group of women who then responded by surrounding me (Get off me!) in an attempt to hug me and persuade me that Jesus loved me. I told them that I was sure he did, but I had no intention of being saved yet again, and could someone please give me a lift back to my home?

The sinner got her lift home. Thank you, Jesus.

49

An Angel called Sam

Angels can appear in many forms.

I believe I encountered one when I was working part-time in the restaurant to support my living expenses while I was at art school. His name was Sam, he was the curly haired Cockney blonde barman at my work and I fell in love with his charm the moment I met him.

Despite his very rough back-ground, Sam had a heart of gold and was incredibly emotionally intelligent. I felt safe in his company. We shared a wonderful back and forth banter from behind the bar to the kitchen. First and foremost he was my friend. He was a fair bit older than me (why spoil the pattern?) and he had a really colourful history.

These were the stories he told me. I had no reason to doubt them then but in retrospect, I realise he may have been telling me entertaining stories that may or may not have been based in reality. For the sake of putting you in the mindset of where I was as a 19- year-old gullible teenager, I'll relay them to you as they were told to me at the time.

He came from Kilburn in North London, the son of a woman who was an active member of the IRA. He told me he had been a feral child, he'd had to learn all the social niceties like using cutlery and reading and writing as an older teenager. Somehow he had slipped under the radar of Social Services growing up.

His past employment history was as rich as his family was poor. In his previous job he had taken on the position of croupier on a cruise ship, had a few too many drinks on the job, went behind the bar and gave the entire bar contents away for free. He was a bit like an intoxicated Cockney version of Robin Hood. The police were waiting to arrest him when the ship docked, and he ended up doing a stint in prison for theft, before escaping and joining the Foreign Legion! (I know, this tale is growing taller every second, and I'm almost embarrassed that my younger self just took it on face value.) The Foreign Legion didn't suit him either, so he went AWOL and, of course, that meant he had to keep moving.

If ADHD had a blonde curly wig, its name would be Sam. His impulsive behaviour was legendary, but my rebellious art school girl loved the bones of him.

I met him at a time when I was spiralling dangerously into masochistic behaviour, as the shame I had built up over the years started to manifest and show its face as eroticised self harm. I had secretly started fantasising about being hurt. Sam, my angel, would help me gently and safely explore this shadow.

Once, during an adult play session, (I was now 19) I asked him with all seriousness to use a knife inside me as a sex toy. Everything in my mind at the time was telling me that this was what I wanted. On the outside, it would appear that I was consenting and asking for kink sex play. Sam was not about to allow me to hurt myself, consent or no consent. Instead, he calmly and coolly tied me up in silence, then blindfolded me and told me he was going to leave me to think about that request for a little while. Then he made out that he had left the room, but I could still feel his presence quietly sitting with me while I worked through what I had just asked for and came to my senses. He made sure I was safe, he didn't judge or act shocked. He was patient, kind, and clever. Of course, when the time came for the blindfold to be removed, I cried my heart out, sobbing like a little child into his chest. He held me gently in his arms and rocked me, kissing the top of my head.

I ended up moving in with Sam at my boss's house for a two-week period during the Summer break from college. Those were heady days. Such wonderfully decadent, sensual memories of working until the early morning hours together, then coming home to an indulgent breakfast of steak, oysters, and tequila. There would be arm fulls of daffodils after making love until it was time to return to work once more.

Once returning to college, I would walk around totally sleep-deprived but fully loved up, painting my face to match the leopard spots on my 80s corseted cotton dress in typical Leigh Bowery fashion.
It was the best of times when it wasn't totally awful.

The young seem to have enormous capacity to burn the candle at both ends and at that point I was giving that candle my brightest flame. My world came crashing in once more when there was talk that the police were catching up with Sam's whereabouts once more. It was time, once again, for him to move on. So I waved goodbye to him at the airport in the messiest, snottiest, drunken tequila-fuelled state and never saw him again.

When you fall... there's always some way you can get back up

Doodle by Imogen

50

Cosplaying Myself

I'm looking at a photo of me taken in my first year at art school. I'm on a weekend visit to my parents, I'm standing on the front porch holding a strange, black, shiny structure, a sculpture I had made in class that week.

It was a deconstructed and reassembled machine (I think I remember it was inspired by a paraffin lamp?) made in different materials, taking its various parts, scaling them up or down to create a brand-new construction. I'd chosen black PVC as my main material, along with cardboard and wadding. The finished piece looked nothing like the original lamp, with its padded tubular structures and random orifices made in shiny black PVC. My naive self had no idea why my lecturers liked this creation so much, but I did notice them exchanging strange, familiar smiles when looking at it. Now I realise I'd subconsciously created some sort of bizarre kink fetish object.

I'm dressed in an outfit of my own creation, consisting of a black chiffon drawstring handkerchief hemmed skirt. It had a white feather print, and I'd laboriously cut out leaf shaped colourful pieces of fabric, edge stitched them all and hand sewn them on to the skirt, giving a feather or flame effect. On my top half, I wore a black and silver lurex jacket with leg o' mutton sleeves that I had made from a thrifted 70s dress. On my spiked up short hair do, I'd tied around a headband with a big bow on the side, in the height of 80s fashion. Black torn fishnets, topped with luminous yellow ankle socks and flat black leather pumps, finished off the classic 80s look.

My mum must've been appalled. She said nothing.

For years she had controlled what I had worn, so when I hit my teenage years, I longed to express my own sense of identity through my clothing choices. This was easier said than done back then, as I had no money to be able to buy my own clothes.

When Mum met Hennie around this time, I happened upon several discarded suits that I experimented with, Annie Hall style. I even bought a trilby hat with my first-ever earnings from a weekend job, to complete the look.

As soon as I was earning my own money, I found the creative thrill of expressing myself through my attire. I frequented local charity shops and bought up the cheapest, campest and sparkliest things.
I found a blue cotton utility boiler suit that I customised with a giant butterfly on the back, painting my face with a butterfly to match.
That felt right. That felt like me.
The blue butterfly boiler suit became a second skin to me back then, just like my skeleton onesie is for me cur- rently.

I realised that this outfit served a social purpose. It kept creeps and predators away from me and only let in those people who were prepared to look and see beyond the weirdness. It has occurred to me that this was a form of masking in its most literal sense. I was signalling my 'otherness' in this full-body mask, this was soft armour. I was creating the basis of the wearable art career I would later go on to enjoy.

Clothing was a social experiment to me, I took mental notes of other's reactions to me and how it felt when I wore certain socially coded styles. I decided to push this experiment to its limit.

I was visiting my mum on a weekend and borrowed one of her work outfits of beige pleated crêpe skirt, modest white blouse and tweed fitted jacket. I combed my hair flat against my head, normal style, rather than it's usual spiked up punk attitude, then forced my feet into a pair of heels, (the lowest ones I could find) and painted my face in a restrained mask of 'natural' feminine make up.

I looked at myself in the mirror and laughed as I didn't recognise myself. I suppose I was cos-playing a neurotypical person.

My bland self tottered out to my usual pub, making a mental note to document this experience. I was curious to see if my clothing choices made people react differently towards me.

This experience would go down as one of the most short-lived of my social experiments.

I ended up tearing off the crippling high heels and running for home after around thirty minutes of being completely overwhelmed by predatory male attention. I felt like I was raw meat being thrown to a pack of wolves.

That experience marked the first and last time I ever dressed in beige. It seems like my kooky style choices had protected me from harm after all. Moreover, when I dressed in a manner where I felt comfortable, I felt fully me, not like I was having to perform a character.

One of my most precious charity shop finds was a lace 'meringue' style wedding dress. This was a gorgeous over the top dress, with a stretch lace beaded bodice and a multi layered, high camp, flouncy tulle skirt that puffed up around my ears whenever I sat down in it. Wearing this dress was a multi-sensory experience for me. I could live out my Disney princess fantasies but give it my punk edge, with spiked hair and dramatic eyeliner and Doc Martin boots. When I put it on, I felt myself becoming.

Becoming whom? I wasn't sure.

This dramatic dress gave me permission to just be me.

I would often team this dress with a brutal German military green bomber jacket that never left my back in the 80s. It had so many pockets and made me feel powerful. It was a perfect foil for the high camp femininity of the wedding dress.

With my bleached blonde short spiky hair, with crude lines cut into the sides of my head, torn fishnets and Doc Marten boots, I found myself being given the nickname of Sweet Punk at college. I may have looked outwardly fierce, but everyone knew that Diane was the one to look out for everyone.

I would regularly remind the super stoned, talented young men on my course to actually do a bit of work so they could get through the year.

In South Africa at that time, there was good reason young men made the effort to stay in education. Once they completed their education, they faced the dreaded call-up for border duty on the Angola/South Africa border. Whatever happened up there to those young men was really messing with their psyches, as once they returned, they were never the same. They would leave as regular young men and return as shells of their former selves, with empty eyes and a new violent disposition, clearly traumatised and shut down from whatever they were forced to do.

In the early, 80s, it would appear that I was one of only two punks in Cape Town. The other one, Morris, was notorious. He didn't appear to be in education or work, but would be found hanging around various nightclubs in Cape Town dressed to the nines in the latest Vivienne Westwood gear. The rumour was he was an addict, his erratic behaviour certainly suggested that. One evening I encountered him, he dragged me around with him to various fast food outlets to pilfer the entire contents of their sugar bowls on the tables outside. He was seemingly fairly well-off, as his mother would fly back and forth to London to pick up his outfits direct from SEX in the Kings Road. My fascination with Morris was short- lived. His energy did not feel safe, plus his lifestyle was a million miles away from mine. I left him to scavenge the packets of sugar on his own, dressed in thousands of pounds worth of designer gear.

I do regret missing out on the real punk scene back in England. It did seem like a very exciting time. Clearly, being a punk in Cape Town wasn't quite the same.

You've just read a portrait in words of the late teenager me, creating, flourishing, exploring and discovering new aspects of herself by being at art school. This expansion would soon come to an abrupt halt when my mother found out that I was serious about a new boyfriend I had met, and he'd moved in with me in my student digs. Mum was to pull all funding and force me to leave art school, but not without push back from my tutors.

My fellow students tried to raise money for me to pay for art materials to help me stay on, and my tutors begged me to take my mother to court to sue her for the completion of my education. They argued that I was at a crucial stage of my development and only had six months remaining before I graduated. They even took me out for dinner in their attempts to persuade me to pursue this course of action.

I just couldn't. The idea of going up against the Mother Monster in court was just too much. I still felt the echoes of the slap. You Bitch! There was no way I could rise up against her.

The boyfriend/husband and me the day I left Art School

So that was that.

I left and took up a permanent post at my Saturday job picture framing shop while my boyfriend continued his studies at the nearby university art school.

Bye Bye Art School. Bye Bye Sally Bowles.

There's a pattern emerging. If only I could see it.

Part 6 There's No Place Like Home

Signposts, Signs and Synchronicities

Row, row, row your boat, gently down the stream
Merrily, merrily, merrily, merrily,
Life is but a dream.

I didn't know it at the time, but this simple children's rhyme would turn out to be a powerful teaching mantra for me in my later years.

Here I am, an explosion of firework ribbons in my hair, sparkly sequinned top and beribboned gypsy style skirt, bashing a tambourine, jumping up and down, enchanting numerous toddlers and tiny humans for the fourth time this weekend.

This is my day job, I am a children's entertainer, face painter and puppeteer and I use my silly skills, farty noises and ability to hold a tune with my loud voice to make my living.

I love it. I specialise in the under fives and I have gained a great reputation among London's yummy mummies.

At this point in my story, I'd been perfecting the art of silly for almost twenty years. Silly was a serious business to me. My secret weapons were an ugly baby fairy puppet called Fifi and the well-known children's rhyme, Row, row, row your boat. Every little party-goer wanted the opportunity to sit in an imaginary row- boat with a magical and cheeky, feather-headed fairy being and scream when they saw the crocodile.

" If you see a crocodile, don't forget to scream! Aargh! "

By this point, my client list read like a who's who in society: Saudi Royalty, the Delevingne's, newsreaders, rockstars, comedians, reality show celebrities, you just never knew who would be the next person to book.

It didn't matter to me much who you were, as long as you paid on time, the children had a good time and the parents and guests were respectful, I was happy.

At one point, I was mistaken for being part of the Orthodox Jewish community, possibly because of my married surname, Goldie. I started to receive bookings from a very specific part of North London, regularly. I went with it as I do not discriminate, children are children, and they all deserve a fun party. Making sure my arms were covered out of respect, I substituted my beloved piggy puppet, PC Porker, for a Basset Hound whose occupation was normally a postman. He was delighted to step in at short notice.

I came across a fair few cultural clashes as a female owned business.

One dad refused to believe I would be able to face-paint the children in the time I had allocated. He was quite dismissive towards me, almost sneering. This triggered old wounds and I managed to not only prove him wrong in my anger, but I did the best job with time to spare.

I would always be paid in cash by the male head of household. Once, one particular Patriarch refused to hand the cash payment to me after a successful party, asking instead to see my boss so he could pay him. I firmly and politely explained that I was my own boss. He screwed up his face, peeled off a few notes and slapped them reluctantly into my palm. As quickly as my North London bookings started, they stopped. I think someone may have worked out that I wasn't actually Jewish.

I wasn't the right fit for them, that was perfectly fine.

There became a moment where I realised that maybe I had to reconsider whether menopause and being a children's entertainer were compatible. Let me preface this story by saying in my twenty-five years of being in this business, I'd never met a child I didn't like or couldn't win over. The adults were a different story, however...

I had been booked by an Indian family to do a birthday party puppet show for their three-year-old son at a popular pizza place in St John's Wood. The lovely mum had made all the arrangements and welcomed me in to the venue. It all started out so well, family and friends were all gathered around, including grandparents, watching and joining in with the children as I went through my warm-up routine.

The birthday boy was standing off to the side with grandpa, and I noticed they had a packet of uninflated balloons in their hands. I thought nothing of that at first and carried on with my routine. Then I felt a sharp sting on my arm and heard giggling, then another sting, this time on my ear, accompanied by a loud man's cheer.

Oh no you didn't.

I spun around to find the grandpa pinging the uninflated balloons at me and encouraging his little grandson to do the same. That moment didn't sit well with my rising menopausal rage. The combination of sexist provocation and disrespect with plummeting oestrogen levels was too much for me to contain. Mustering up all the self-control I could manage, I calmly turned around, walked behind my puppet show and silently packed away my gear, leaving the audience to think whatever they needed to think. I'd rather that, than risk my rage spilling over mid-performance. I abandoned the show before I'd even begun.

Mum was mortified, and I knew she was in an impossible position. I told her I didn't expect payment, but I was not prepared to be treated in that manner. She paid me anyway, along with profuse apologies. It wasn't her fault. I understood the Patriarchal dynamics of what was happening, but for the sake of my self-respect, this was something I could not tolerate. Being perceived as a clown in a business context is sometimes a tricky thing to navigate, especially as a woman. I'm proud of that memory.

My quarter of a century of being a children's entertainer started quite by chance. I had put on a puppet show for Imogen's 5th birthday.
One of the attending mums told me that she had a friend who did this sort of thing for a living and did I want her details? I met with her, got some tips and pointers and stepped out into the big mad world of being a professional silly person. I had many wonderful times and a fair few miserable ones. The worse one was the party I had to entertain for after receiving the news of my dad's death.

The day before, I had received the news as I was on my way home after a full day's puppeteering. I was squished onto a lower deck bus seat at peak hour. My suitcase of puppets was crammed on my lap. My rainbow explosion of ribbons decorated my hair, and this was all finished off with a bright yellow plastic duck fascinator.
There I was, crying on the phone, on this packed bus, highly visible and looking quite ridiculous with this yellow duck on my head and tears streaming down my cheeks.
The only thing that held me from tipping over into complete hysteria was this duck, it made me super aware of being perceived. I would rather not embarrass myself any further.
This was so aligned with dad's silly spirit. It was as if he'd timed that call made by my uncle, deliberately.
I could hear my dad's voice echoing around my head, "Pack it in, Di, I'm here. Cheer up, duck". (Duck being a Midlands familiar fig-

ure of speech and I chuckled ruefully knowing how much Dad loved a pun.)

At the party the next day, I went through the motions of my silly routine while my heart broke into tiny pieces. A few years later, I would receive a tarot card reading that told me my dad had a message for me from spirit. It was

" Keep being silly, Di, you're going to need it. "

Then very soon after, I got the news of the double suicide of my daughter and son-in-law. Dad's message couldn't have felt more poignant.

In some of my darkest moments of grief, it was silly that rescued me.
Drinking tequila with my dear friend Vince who came to watch Cabaret with me, was a tonic. We ended up drunkenly reenacting the musical numbers in the front room, giggling hysterically as we tried to reenact ' Two Ladies' and camped it up to the title track.
Then the tears came, and it was all perfection.

Imogen's death had forced me into a place of deep surrender, the choice was simple, surrender to the moment and feel, or shut off into denial and numbing. I chose surrender as the lesser of the two evils, as I understood just how much my other daughter and grandchildren were relying on me.

Row row row your boat gently down the stream...
The boat of life, of experiences, flows down the stream, following the current following the one-way pull of birth to death, (note I didn't say life to death, that is significant.)
That lifeboat is going to flow downstream whether we row it or not because death is inevitable. Our human condition of being ego-

driven creatures means that we enjoy the feeling of being involved in our lives. So the rhyme encourages us to row gently because, actually, we don't need to row at all.

In surrender, when we let go of the oars completely, we get to lie back and watch all the beautiful scenery on the banks of the river. We can then notice the signposts and messages that are there to help guide us through life.

We also get to notice the other boats in the river, with their crews desperately paddling upstream against the current, to no avail. They are busy going nowhere. All that effort to stand still. Worse still, they miss all the signposts along the river bank as they sweat and focus on beating the flow of the current, ending up exhausted and being taken with the current eventually anyway.

You may as well give up the fight.

Merrily, merrily, merrily, merrily, life is but a dream

This is a direct instruction to follow your joy and try to stay as happy as possible because life is but a dream, a mere projection of our thoughts. This is even found in Quantum Theory.

The father of Quantum Mechanics, Max Planck stated,

"When you change the way you look at things, the things you look at change."

This was later popularised by Wayne Dyer, author, speaker, and teacher.

It is possible to collectively dream up a new world, and the instructions of this extraordinary potential seem to be hidden in plain sight in a nursery rhyme.

Isn't this just beautiful?

Since my moment of surrendering to life and lying back in my boat as it floats gently downstream, I've been bombarded with signs, synchronicities, and symbols. Sometimes so forceful, you could almost describe their force of wanting to be noticed as rude or violent, sometimes even comical.

Even before I surrendered, there were clues, pointers to the pointers, if you will. My pattern seeking brain would observe these pointers and ascribe meaning to them, navigating my life's direction to a very specific destination.

I was a second year at art school, and I was thoroughly enjoying living life on my terms, free from the prison of demands that was my life living with my parents. In my new shared flat, I could live life the way I wanted. The very first night I moved into my new flat, I slept fully clothed, boots and all, on top of my bedding, with headphones on listening to Pink Floyd's Dark Side of the Moon just because I could. There was no-one to tell me not to. This felt delicious in a way that is hard for me to describe.

My wardrobe by then reflected my new-found freedom, as I'd collected an eclectic bunch of second hand clothes that reflected my personality. My favourite outfit had to be my wedding dress and army jacket combination, though. It was when, dressed in my signature look, I found myself sitting across a table in a dark pub. I would soon be telling a man that I had just met, who was to become my future husband and father to my two beautiful daughters, to kiss me.

I had managed to get myself an admirer at this point, not that it was wanted or encouraged. We had met back in my Green house days, he was a friend of the family. I hadn't really noticed his interest in me until he started turning up at my picture framing shop that was my weekend job. He would hang around until my shift ended, then just follow me around like a lost puppy. At this point, I had no idea how to address this very awkward situation, boundaries were not my strong point as a late teen, so I just let him tag along.

I stopped off to get changed out of my work clothes into my wedding /army jacket combo, then headed off to the local pub with my benign stalker. Perhaps he would leave me alone in the pub, where there were other people to distract his attention?

We sat in the back in the gloomiest, darkest part of the pub and I ordered the student essential, a bottle of Tassenberg, a cheap, locally produced full-bodied red wine. After three glasses, my puppy was out cold in a pool of his vomit, head slumped on the table. I was worried, disgusted, relieved and surprised.

I cleaned up the mess, checked on his breathing and left him to sleep it off on the velvet bunk bench.

The previous day, my flatmate, Monique and I had ventured out to the final year art show at the nearby art school, Michaelis, which was the prestigious art wing of University of Cape Town.

It was a 'proper' art school, not like our college.

I was curious to see the art that came out of the posh art school, so I dressed up and headed off.

I was bitterly disappointed in the art I saw there. Trawling through studio after studio in the Fine Art department, I clambered up and down stairs, seeking something that would punch me in the guts or tickle my senses. But all I saw were vast swathes of what I found to be emp- ty, meaningless conceptual pieces.

I understand that art is subjective, I learned that none of this art resonated with me.

I headed downstairs to the free bar, (big boxes of wine). After all, that is the place where most poor art students are to be found. Just before I got there I made a last-minute detour and headed in to the graphic design department, maybe out of curiosity as graphic design was what I thought I'd be doing a few years back.

There it was!
The sucker punch to the gut I'd been looking for...

In front of me were some darkly disturbing and eerily fascinating collage pieces depicting the upcoming digital age and its impact on humans. There was a strange, warped, big-headed tech guy sitting at his computer, tapping the key- board with weird pointy fingers.

The way this illustration was put together was deeply and darkly fascinating. There was a deep sense of nihilism emanating from these images, of which David Lynch and Francis Bacon would be proud.

I stood transfixed in front of this work in absolute awe, tinged with revulsion. That was what I had been looking for. That was real art.

I'd found it ironically in the graphic design department.

I chuckled internally as my brain registered that this person was creating fine art in the graphic design department in a school for fine art, and I was doing fine art in a school mostly geared up for graphic design.

Feeling satisfied that I'd found the feeling I'd been looking for, I headed out to the wine boxes once again.

As I poured my glass of red wine, I could feel eyes on me.

I turned around and there was this very tall, skinny, dark haired young man, all dressed in black except for a wine coloured neckerchief tied rakishly around his neck. It suited his tumbling dark curls and piercing, cold blue eyes that I couldn't help notice were staring at me over the rim of his wine glass.

I took a mental note of this handsome person and described him to Monique when I got back to the flat.

"Oh, that's Mike", she said,
" He's a friend of my mate, I'll introduce you guys next time."

My tummy did a little somersault as I wondered when this next time could be arranged.

Back to the darkness of the pub. I'm staring into the abyss (myopically as I was too vain to wear my very much needed glasses) in my embarrassment of being out with this drunken puppy dog, then out of the gloom there appeared a familiar tall, skinny figure, dressed in black with long dark ringlets and those piercing blue eyes. He sat down at my table, directly opposite me. In my panic and slightly inebriated state, my brain told me that This must be a dream. In dreams, you can say or do what you like, so I did.

I blurted out, "Kiss me!"
To my surprise, he did. In retrospect, this is absolutely the most confusing part of this tale, Mike was not known for public displays of affection. We started to chat. I told him of my experience of the previous evening's exhibition, as I figured that was common ground we shared. I described in great detail the work I had been transfixed by in the graphic design department, the work that had restored my faith in art. He smiled, there was a pause and he said,
"That's my work."
It turned out I had been staring at him the whole time I was sat at the table, ac-
cording to his friends sat at the table opposite. Because of my feeble eyesight with- out my glasses, I had not seen anyone in the gloom of the dark pub. His friends had encouraged him to take the hint and go over to the girl in the wedding dress and army jacket. So he did.

A year later, we took an aeroplane back to the UK, and we were married.

Two years later, I gave birth to our first child, Imogen.

Imogen Saskia Goldie, I chose those names for her.

Imogen, because it was a very unusual name at the time, and had connections to literature, as Shakespeare had inadvertently invented it by misspelling Innogen in Cymbeline. It would go on to suit her perfectly.

Saskia was selected as a nod to my favourite artist, Rembrandt. Saskia was his muse and his wife.

After Imogen's premature death, I would be alerted to a message in anagram form in Imogen's name, by a medium. It was this:

I'm gone, A kiss, A God Lie.

I see this as evidence of our soul contract with one another. We agreed to go on this journey together. I would be the mother who was prepared to let her child leave early, and continue to learn from her daughter's teachings once she was in spirit form.

Imogen had always been destined to be my teacher and my ancestor.

A chalked message found on the pavement after Imogen's death near her sister's home

Before she decided to check out, she'd had a conversation with her father, who'd told her not to join the infamous 27 club. She never saw a full day of 28 as she took her life on her 28th birthday.

Her music, however, will live on eternally and her spirit continues to tease me with its full-body goosebump hugs.

51

The God Lie

Ever since the mystery led me to discover the message encoded deep in Imogen's name:

I'm gone, a kiss, a God lie, I've been curious as to the meaning of that final phrase : a God lie.

I know this is at the root of the reason for our shared mission, don't ask me how I know, I just do. It would be like me asking you to prove the presence of a higher power, you just know.

At first, I used my pattern seeking brain to connect the God lie to the Patriarchal teachings of modern Christianity. This was created by the deletion of female centred texts, such as the Gospel of Mary, within the early Christian movement and the emerging Catholic Church. This deliberate censored engineering of these sacred texts has resulted in a very unbalanced narrative that silences the voices of women and creates the sort of God that requires us to prostrate ourselves in sinful unworthiness before him. We need to be forgiven before we can enter the kingdom of heaven.

This transactional version of our relationship with a higher power I believe has led to a way of controlling the masses, especially women, keeping us subdued and unworthy.

The first representation of woman is Eve. She becomes the temptress of Adam, leading him to his expulsion from God's favour, not forgetting that Eve was created from a part of Adam rather than being created in the magical portal that is the womb.

I believe that the truth of it all is that we are all part of God, the Oneness. Everything vibrates with the energy of the divine. Consciousness is the manifestation of God in everything. Even a stone has a form of consciousness, albeit a very densely vibrating one.

In John 14:1, Jesus even states himself that everyone can perform miracles like him.

For a while this explanation of the God lie held me, it seemed to be the message I was looking for. Today, things shifted after I watched a documentary about the controversial Christian mega church, Hillsong. Now I believe the God lie goes deeper.

What I witnessed in this documentary, was a cult-like organisation sweeping the globe using the name of Jesus and the same methodology used by the Scientologists, to make an enormous amount of money through brainwashing techniques and coercive control.

Jesus was clearly big business.

The founder of this mega church was a felon, wanted in his home country, Australia, for human trafficking crimes. He had run to the USA, who had embraced him wholeheartedly. Maybe, perhaps because their President was also a convicted felon, he'd found a sympathetic, like-minded sanctuary there. His cult-like church has certainly flourished, becoming the church that many celebrities endorse, with its arena stagings complete with dramatic pyro- technic displays.

This group reminded me of my experience with the Rhodes Memorial church cult people, where they'd tried and failed to recruit me as a teen. I wondered if this was the same group in their early stages.

A quick google revealed that Hillsong has a forceful presence in Cape Town currently so it is quite plausible that I had been at one of their earliest meetings at Rhodes Memorial. The cult-like structure and tithing systems would suggest it was one and the same.

I pondered at the aligning of this Pentecostal style mega church with the political right. US President Trump's survival of an assumed assassination attempt (I believe it was staged but that's another book) used as proof of divine intervention of God himself, rather like the Catholic Pope claiming to have direct access to God.

The way MAGA culture works is very reminiscent of a cult. There is very little wonder why this cult like church style and MAGA fit like hand in glove.

There is one glaring problem though. Jesus, the man at the centre of it all, would not have approved of these churches or the bigoted thought processes of MAGA followers.

Christ Consciousness is about unconditional love and acceptance, not hate and bigotry.

Christ embraced the poor, the outcasts, the sick, women, and children and those who society deems unacceptable.

This is the biggest God lie of them all: Jesus is being sold as a bigot.

52

Marriage, Motherhood and Me

I have a complicated relationship with the institution of marriage. There's the deep ancestral cultural pull from my Romany heritage towards it, with clear Patriarchal conditioning that taught me, primarily through Disney adaptations of traditional fairy tales, that to be married is a woman's ultimate achievement. To be chosen by a man as his life partner was the highest accolade in our society for a woman.

The threat of becoming an 'old maid', unwanted, unloved and left alone with cats or dogs as her only company, hung over our heads, spurring us on to find our Prince Charming and avoid such a disgraceful fate. I was told and taught that it was every little girl's birthright to be a Queen-for-a-day. It has always puzzled me why girls and women focus all their hopes and dreams on one single day, where they wear a white dress. How does going through all these rituals validate their worth as wo- men? There's a party afterwards, that is fun, but I'm not sure a life of drudgery is worth one fun night dancing and merry making. Whatever happens after that one day isn't relevant, apparently. Surely, it is every woman's birthright to be a Queen every day?

Before I had an awakening and understood my worth as a human in her own right, I felt and responded to that pull to surrender the sovereignty of my person-hood.

I found myself standing next to a trembling, tall man in a bright orange room that was the Brixton registry office back in the mid-80s. I said,

"I do,"

as my dad looked on as our witness. I was wearing a deep purple shot taffeta vintage dress that I'd found in Camden market. From a distance, it may have looked like I got married in black. My ring was a simple, cheap band of nine-carat gold, it was all we could afford.

My wedding cake was a gift from my employer, the head chef at the Sloane Square Hotel. I was the only woman working in the kitchen at the hotel, making cold food and salads for the wine bar, and I was responsible for the food displays. The head chef and I got along really well, sharing a laddish banter between us, a vital form of communication in such a male dominated space that is a professional kitchen. Chef had heard I was getting married and had promised to make me a cake. When he presented it to me, I laughed. A simple round white iced cake sported a large purple penis in the centre with cream ejaculate oozing out of the tip, two chocolate profiterole testicles and the word "Bollocks" written in purple icing across the remaining space.

Looking back now, maybe I should have taken offence at such a vulgar cake, with its chauvinist insensitivity. At the time, I just found it funny.

I remember taking it back on the tube to our tiny shared room in our hostel and feeling rather proud. I suppose that irreverent attitude towards marriage suits the way I view it now as a divorced woman.

Marriage would not suit me in my present incarnation as a wild, free, unmasked, proud local eccentric weirdo witch, complete with old dog familiar.

Back then, marriage served my needs in a strange but useful way.

For the next sixteen years, marriage would be my safe place to disappear and play the role I needed to play. Whilst I had the picket fence of the normal, respectable Mrs status around me, I was free of the shame of Jezebel. I was also gaining the approval of my mum, who was now thrilled I was a respectably married woman.

My art ambitions were mostly left behind as a sacrificial lamb on the altar of respectability and I traded in my wacky clothes for a uniform of mostly jeans and tee- shirts. Occasionally, I would break out of uniform and don a heavy cotton and lace bloomer and petticoat set that I'd found at a theatrical costumes sale, but still my style was toned right down now I was a married woman.

This was no romantic love story, however. There was no heartfelt bended-knee proposal. In its place, a rather logical discussion where we agreed it was necessary for us to be married so that he could stay in England and avoid having to return to South Africa and the threat of border duty.

Did he love me?

Looking back, I'm inclined to say no. I think I was very useful for him, and then I became a habit and responsibility, especially after the birth of our two daughters. I had a very skewed radar for what love felt like at this point.

The biggest demand I had placed on myself was the belief that I had made my bed, so I had better lie in it. I had committed so now I had to follow through, no matter what.

It would be hellish, and I would feel like I was drowning, but I would stick it out stubbornly.

Once I fell pregnant, (totally unintentionally) the determination to make the marriage work became even stronger as I didn't want my children to be the product of a broken marriage as I was, so I locked myself in even further. I was going to push through and fix the situation in whatever way I could.

My solution to fixing what was to become a very troubled and fairly loveless marriage, was to lean in to being a mum. I let go of all my personal needs, supporting my husband and raising my children, in opposition to the way my mother raised me.

No matter what life threw at me, I was determined to show unconditional love towards my daughters. I was determined to do it right.

I continued to draw as my lifeline to sanity as the pressures of motherhood, marriage, and poverty piled on. My breast- feeding baby would be in the crook of one arm, and I'd be drawing her with the other.

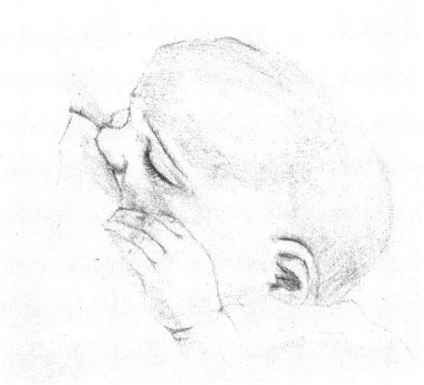

I took every opportunity to draw the babies when they were sleeping.

I managed to paint every now and then and the painting reflected my state of mind.

These little glimmers of joy kept me going through brutally tough times. Margaret Thatcher spoke about how hard work would pay off on our 6-inch portable black and white television, and I would throw things at the screen. She had no concept of how it felt to have a new baby with no furniture except a mattress on the floor and upturned cardboard boxes for tables. My new husband could not claim any social security benefits due to his immigration status. I'd lost out on any maternity benefits as my lovely hotel job had ended up exploiting me while I was pregnant. I was forced to quit because carrying heavy buckets of cold food up and down stairs while heavily pregnant and nauseous was not something I could continue to do safely. They should have offered me alternative positions in the hotel whilst I was pregnant. We weren't allowed to join a union. Even though I had been awarded the Employee of the Year prize, the previous year, the HR team didn't seem to care that I was a sobbing mess at the end of every shift. So I was forced to quit. Because I had quit, I lost out on Maternity pay. Consequently, we were as poor as it got. No amount of hard work would dig us out of this penury.

Five years later, after the birth of my second daughter, we'd managed to find our feet somewhat. I'd set myself up as a children's entertainer, and my husband had used his compositional skills and trained up as a television editor.

We'd been lucky enough to have been given a council flat, being a homeless new mum was our terrifying and precarious route to that.

We were able to build up gradually to create a cosy home for our small family.

My firstborn was challenging as a baby. She screamed non-stop from the day she was brought home from the hospital. She rarely smiled, and I called her my ' old soul '.

My second baby, Allegra, was an entirely different baby, full of smiles and chunky, milky contentment.

I'd taken up sewing soft sculpture body forms as the babies grew as I realised I couldn't paint with my focus being so divided. I needed to be able to sink into the zone, uninterrupted to paint and having two children under 5, that was never going to be possible.

Imogen and Mummy's sculpture

S ewing these weird busts seemed to scratch the creative itch for a while and I could create in manageable bursts of creativity.

M y husband managed to find himself a large studio space in a nearby art collective. I remember helping him prepare his studio space, down on my hands and knees scrubbing the parquet floor. Now I look back with confusion as to how I could so readily accept such a secondary role and not claim my own agency as an artist. I'm certainly making up for it now.

This is what marriage did to me. It slowly eroded my sense of self, until by the end, I was left bereft of any tangible concept of who I was. The confident, creative, chaotic, charismatic girl that had kissed a stranger in a dark bar, had become a biddable, mousy, confused and bland wife. A wife who was prepared to stand outside the designer shop upon instruction from her husband, waiting for him to finish buying his designer underwear. His wife, dressed in charity shop clothes, was too shabby to be seen with him.

I had become an embarrassment to him and myself. That is what I had allowed myself to become. Was it my own rigidity and need to stick to rules that had created this creature that I no longer recognised as myself? Or was it something else outside my own doing?

That night I journaled about my day as a storm raged outside, and I cried as I realised something had to change.

Where had Diane gone?

Echoes of my mother's voice across the generational divide. Where's Sandra gone?

53

Millennium

The year 2000, Millennium, what a moment in time that was for me.

My husband had stocked up the kitchen cupboards with tins and jars, torches, matches, and batteries and all sorts of survival supplies in response to the fear of the Millennium Bug, a potential digitally induced apocalypse that just never happened.

I remember walking with him and our two girls, 12 and 9, to the banks of the Thames at Vauxhall Bridge, to watch the New Year's Eve firework spectacular. This year it was guaranteed to be even more spectacular than ever. It was Imogen's 12th birthday too so we should have all been in a celebratory mood, but I distinctly remember feeling deep emptiness, knowing that things in our family were about to change dramatically.

The feared apocalypse would turn out to be much closer to home.

That night sticks in my memory as we joined thousands of excited revellers as they lined the banks of the river, many of us heading directly onto the muddy shore of the river bank. We laughed as we witnessed person after person losing their shoes in the deep, sticky suction of the water logged mud.

When the fireworks began (this year would be the first digitally designed firework display creating flowers and other symbols in the night sky) I remember feeling a deep sense of emptiness even though my emotions were heightened in awe and wonder at the noisy visual display. Tears rolled down my cheeks, and they quickly turned into sobs, I could not explain to myself or anyone else why I found myself in such an emotional state.

That was the moment I knew I needed to start again.

Not long after, I told our daughters that mummy and daddy were divorcing.

Imogen and Allegra were outwardly calm, but who knows what emotions were coursing through their bodies? I felt like the world's biggest failure as a mum as here I was repeating history, breaking up our family just like my mum had broken up mine and for Imogen, at the same age.

My girls were entirely unique creatures. Imogen, the older by three years, was outwardly reserved, quiet, studious, serious, socially awkward, (some might describe her as a loner). A perfectionist, she never had to be told what to do, she always just did it, a vegetarian from babyhood by choice (I tried to give her meat as a toddler, but she persistently rejected it) a lover of beige food, a fiercely funny character with a well-developed sense of silly.

She was a furious dancer, she was earnest about her dancing to her favourite tunes as a toddler (anything by the Stranglers would send her running for her dancing outfit, consisting of a woolly elephant decorated hat, and her 'dancey' skirt that was an elasticated white cotton frilly skirt).

Once she was appropriately attired she would get down to the serious business of grooving, knees bent, elbows akimbo and furiously twisting to the beat.

She was an avid consumer of books, these days I think she'd be described as hyperlexic. Words and stories made her happy (like her mum), she wrote incredible pieces of fiction, she received a grade of one hundred percent for a piece of writing at secondary school. She was an avid notebook collector and user and journalled constantly.

It would be in one of these notebooks left behind, that she had squirrelled away in my cupboards before she left for Cambodia, that I would find this story she wrote at the age of 20.

The Strange Story of the Mothenfolk

A married couple in their late forties had one day come to the conclusion that in their dissatisfaction with human life, it would be better for them to become moths. Despite being parents of two children, A girl aged 11 and a boy aged 8, they were to pursue their dream with the help of a recent scientific breakthrough that allowed them both to shrink down considerably in size and sprout fully functional wings. The only downside to this being they would no longer be able to communicate with other humans, their children included of course. The couple accepted this eventuality as small sacrifice for the peace and freedom of moth-like existence. The children would have to find a way to cope without them and would likely grow up to be strong, independent adults. So one Tuesday evening the woman cooked a filling, nutritious meal for her son and daughter and went upstairs with her husband to commence the necessary cocooning stage of their transformation. Hungry and in good spirits, the children arrived home from school an hour later to a seemingly empty house. Cautiously and with a degree of anxiety, they called out for their parents, searching to no avail. Sadly resigned yet curious as to their parents whereabouts, they settled down for dinner in their oddly quiet dining room. They sat next to each other, eating peas one at a time until they lost interest in eating and headed off to bed.

The next morning they awoke and found their parents as normal, sitting calmly in the living room. Their father watching television and their mother reading a gardening magazine. They silently agreed not to bring up the previous evening and instead settled, relieved, for breakfast before leaving for school.

The woman sighed heavily as she read an editorial piece on shed lighting. The cocooning had not gone successfully, evidently and they were expecting a tele- phone call from the metamorphosis clinic that afternoon to discuss what further actions they were to take and whether human to moth metamorphosis was right for them. The man sighed too as he had become rather obsessed with the idea. To be a moth, they thought with great longing, was surely the purest of states. How he hungered for soft, fluttering flights in the moonlight, towards each awesome glowing orb he spied. He certainly felt he was mentally ready even to the point of losing some cognitive human abilities. He had even bumped repeatedly without realising it against the neon sign of a kebab shop just yesterday. Yes, he urged quietly to himself, I am ready. His wife, however was not so steadfast in her belief, she feared for the fate of her children, even though she saw metamorphosis as the best way out of her unutterably desperate state of depression. Her feelings of worthlessness had not extended themselves on to her feelings for her beautiful son and daughter. If only they were older, she wished. Maybe then I could let myself slip slowly into moth-hood without the slightest echo of a doubt that what I would be doing would be beautiful, because she truly believed it would be beautiful. The clinic called shortly and listened to their concerns intently. "Of course," the doctor on the phone explained, "you are not fully prepared for metamorphosis. In refusing to cocoon successfully," he continued, "their bodies had voiced their disapproval. More therapy was needed to convince the physical and mental selves to cooperate."

The father was somewhat angry that all the readiness within him had not been sufficient. He argued bullishly with the doctor until he was tired of being angry and then retired early to bed.

The woman tightened the bandages around the sore stumps of her fingers of her left hand, worried that she would bleed too much and risk a repeated failure which she didn't feel she could take. Another patient at the *metamorphosis clinic undergoing his seventh attempt had warned her about the hazards of doubt, how when he had felt at his strongest and most moth-like, it was a momentary lapse of connection whilst amputating his remaining upper thigh, a flash of mere human emotion that had pulled him right back to the beginning. It's this or that terrible emptiness, she assured herself, before pressing herself to her husband and turning out the light.*

The children had not forgotten about that night of a quite unsettling nature for they had in the past weeks become aware of things that concerned them. Each night at the family dinner in front of the television, the two children would glance nervously up at their parents as they attempted to eat their food normally. By now the parents only had a forefinger and thumb each, the rest of their hands tightly covered in dark bandages. They dared not ask but the sight was shocking. Boy and girl gazed simultaneously as the father dropped his fork laden with mashed potato, sighed and slowly went down to pick it up. His feet shuffled rigidly as he leaned. The children looked at each other in confusion; both their mother and father's shoes were stuffed with pieces of cereal box wedged between their feet and their shoes like doorstops. Their father looked at them sternly and the children rapidly resumed eating. They couldn't imagine why such strange habits had befallen their parents. Every night they'd whisper through the sides of their bunk-bed to one another,

"Maybe they're shrinking?" the boy speculated one night, but his observation was met with silence.

The woman was struggling to maintain her sadness for her children. Her slow feeling of distance from them hurt her like it was they who had turned against her. The pain was deep but it was not unfamiliar to her. She had concluded that the way she could eventually let go would be to ignore their existence. So far it seemed they had not even questioned their odd behaviour, which hurt her more, but she endured and remained sadly resigned to her fate.

Her husband had become blank, childlike in his mentality and incapable of much at all. His sleep was interrupted by strange dreams of falling and being a limbless torso like the man they had met in the clinic. This image scared him as much as it inspired him. He felt the promise of moth life edging ever closer, engulfing him like a mountain of heavy blankets, suffocating him almost. His wife would be woken in the early hours of the night by his stifled cries of "Ehr, ehr." His struggles to accept his passive state audible to the children also who often dreamed about their parents crawling across the floor, like caterpillars, their whole bodies bandaged and tight.

B arely three months later, the woman had lost the fight. Her husband woke to find her grappling with the window in panic, nudging it meekly with her shoulders and grunting. Hobbling out of bed he went over and rested his cheek on her back until she had calmed.

"No more" he pleaded and she nodded.

That night they left and drove to the Dover cliffs, their children twitching in their

    sleep, cocooned in their sheets like pupas.

I mogen's other entries in her numerous journals contained her many obsessions. Even from a very young age, she would dedicate an entire book to her love for the alternative cabaret noir band, the Tigerlillies, the surreal humour of comedy duo Vic and Bob and later

The Mighty Boosh. She was also a talented artist from a very young age, free and wild in her expression, curiously lacking the usual crippling self consciousness that often prevents young children from expressing themselves artistically. It seemed there was nothing that Imogen couldn't do. Except perhaps for her struggles to relate to her sister, Allegra.

I would observe my beautiful, vivacious ray of sunshine, Allegra (named because she was born at a brisk pace, and she had a ready smile for everyone she met) desperately struggle to get some reciprocating emotion from her big sister. Allegra was her big sister's shadow, wherever Imogen went, Allegra was sure to be right behind her. Whereas Imogen was socially reserved, Allegra appeared to be the complete opposite, readily making friends with strangers with her warm smile and sunny disposition. She was the cutest child, with twinkling mischievous eyes and a tousled mop of blonde curls. She was a very affectionate child and a very easy-going baby, at first, I put down their differences in their babyhoods as second baby syndrome as I was clearly more relaxed as a mum the second time around. Where I would struggle to get any sort of hug from Imogen, Allegra would run and jump into my arms at every pick up time at primary school. Allegra was a bright and capable child, but I soon saw that she didn't understand her abilities. It must have been very difficult to be in the shadow of her big sister, who had set the impossibly high gifted standard. I'm not a pushy parent, I want my children to want to engage with whatever brings them joy, I know that learning is a lifelong endeavour and not the sum-total of what you achieve in school.

Allegra would go on to prove this marvellously by being the first in the family to graduate from University, qualifying as a midwife a few years after losing her big sister. Because Imogen was clearly so socially awkward and really struggled to engage with friends, (many people really admired her but found her challenging to get to know), Allegra's social struggles remained masked. I would observe the various fallouts and squabbles in Allegra's social life and I would simply put it down to a difficult year group, never once considering that the struggle may have been Allegra's. She had a strong independent will from a very young age. My mother, after meeting her 4-year-old granddaughter for the first time, declared to me that I should crush Allegra's spirit before it got out of control. I was mortified and shocked at her words and I replied absolutely not, that she would need that fierce spirit in the future, especially as a girl. How right I was.

My extraordinary Allegra would grow up to become my closest friend and the woman I would continue to admire the most in life.

Being a single mum after divorce was challenging. I presumed that all family stuff would be regarded equally in the system, and that each parent would be held equally to account by law for both the financial and emotional wellbeing of their children.
After all, even though we were no longer spouses, we still continued to be parents, nothing changes that.
Diane met Patriarchy like a slap in the face from her mother.

Bitch! Wake up!

Before divorce, I had no knowledge or interest in feminism. Pretty soon afterwards, I would find myself in a state of righteous indignation. I realised that fathers, should they choose, could just walk away into the sunset (or in his case, a round the world trip to Australia and Las Vegas, sending back the children trinkets) declare themselves bankrupt, and never have to engage with their children again, effectively becoming emotionally and financially immune. I naively thought the family court system would have things in place to prevent this happening, but no, I was wrong.

Ladies, mums, divorce at your peril, especially if you can't afford legal representation. I'd heard that people can be radicalised through intense life experience, I never expected divorce would create the feminist in me. I consoled myself that my unconditional support of my girls would reap future rewards for our relationships, and mourned the loss of a father figure on my daughters' behalf.

We did later arrange weekend visits and some financial support, but it was to be short-lived once he went on to have more children," The boys he'd always wanted" with his next partner.

Imogen would never come to terms with this and would point-blank refuse to meet her brothers.

54

Dance

Let the music play, I want to dance the night away.

I've just lit a tea light candle to complete a ritual that started two days ago at a weekend dance workshop, Soul Power. It was run by a DJ, artist and movement facilitator, Christian De Sousa, who, like in the song, could be said to have saved my life.

    Eight years ago, I was led through someone who had seen my kimonos on stage worn by Tank and the Bangas, who then contacted the band, asking where he could get one for himself. He consequently came to my home, and after finding a piece that resonated with him, said he was off to dance in a church in Vauxhall.

    By this point, he had heard the story of my lovely Imogen, my grief being very fresh, anyone who entered my home would be subject to her absence of presence. My ears pricked up, dance in a church? That sounded like it was meant for me, coming at the perfect time when I needed it the most. Dancing had always been the source of my emotional regulation, whether I was consciously aware that that was what I was doing, or not. It would soothe my soul to be able to get lost in the centre of the music.

This messenger sent from source, suggested I come along to Vauxhall St Peter's church whenever I had a free Thursday evening and give it a try.

Signposts and synchronicities strike yet again.
This particular church had already been part of my story.
I had, at one point, a temporary, freezing cold and not terribly practical, art studio space inside this church. The vicar at the time was fairly progressive, and she was interested in different ways of bringing the community into the church. Experimental booth style spaces were created down the sides of the huge central hall of the church and offered out to local artists and crafts people at a very reasonable rate. At the time, I was making soft sculptures and I had the intention of focusing on sewing in the church. Unfortunately, it didn't really work out, as my fingers were always too numb from cold to sew.

The next time I had an encounter with this extraordinary space with its high vaulted ceiling, stained-glass windows, gilded altar and carpeted floor, was not so wholesome but probably far more exciting to recall.

I was deep in divorce proceedings, but we had been invited as a couple to a wedding of friends of my soon-to-be ex-husband. The wedding and reception were to be held in the church at Vauxhall St Peters. Maintaining the historical connection with the nearby Pleasure Gardens, the theme was set as the 18th Century and guests were invited to dress accordingly.
My creative spark immediately reignited.
I've always appreciated a good dress up challenge. I set about creating a corseted crinoline dress from a pair of heavy damask curtains I'd

found in the charity shop. I paired the dress with a cheap white blonde wig that I fashioned into a powdered up do, complete with bird in birdcage, nestled within. Powdering my face and décolletage and painting on some black beauty spots and red lips, I felt the part.

For the first time in many years, I felt like myself, even though my reflection showed something more reminiscent of a Baroque lady of the night. Husband hired his hose, waistcoat, and jacket combination from the costume shop along with dresses for the girls. We all attended this very unusual event in this exquisite setting.

Inside, the main hall of the church had been transformed into an indoor version of the Pleasure Gardens as they were in the 18th Century, with topiary, fountains, and formal floral arrangements. It was magical and dream-like. The guests and couple were all seated in the belly of the church, right up against the organ and the golden altar.

Uncharacteristically for me, I cried at the ceremony, the tears making watery salty tracks down my white powdered cheeks as the poignancy of my witnessing a new marriage whilst in the throes of dissolving my own became quite overwhelming. By this point, we had separated, and the girls were due to be spending time at their dad's house for the weekend.

During the reception, in the faux interior Pleasure Gardens, I had spotted a particular gentleman who had stood out from the other male guests as this dandy gentleman had come dressed head to foot in black as a Highwayman. Without giving too much away, we would end up adventuring that weekend together, involving the Royal Vauxhall Tavern (he was clearly a well-known face there) and some very body and soul affirming safe play. After feeling completely invisible for 15 years (and also completely faithful) it felt good to be seen again.

Thank you, handsome Highwayman.

St Peter's church would welcome me back in a new way as I discovered 5 Rhythms dance, the magic carpet and how this practice would offer me a place of pure acceptance and a safe space to be fully me. Led by Christian, Sweaty Thursdays would become the highlight of my week. I would queue up with around 150 others to dance with abandon on the magic carpet with the other sweaty, expressive souls. We'd all follow the music as it took us on a journey through flow, staccato, chaos, lyrical and finally stillness where my brain would be completely silent.

In this quiet place, I would find my body performing its slow and alchemical dance of grief. I found my happy, flappy hands in my very first experience of the dance, my suppressed hand stim from babyhood. My fingers and whole body exploded in an outburst of joy and overwhelming exhilaration as the music poured through me and my body became one with its frequency.

During the closing circle, I shared my story of losing Imogen and how the dance had given me a place to express all the messy feelings that grieving suicide can bring. I was also very moved to realise that had I known earlier about 5 Rhythms, perhaps Imogen would still be here, even though I was acutely aware that I was most probably voicing my feelings from the bargaining phase of grief. This practice has been proven to be completely transformative. I credit it for allowing me a space to explore my rawest emotions in this dance laboratory setting that is the 5 rhythms community. In the words of the song, 'Last night a DJ saved my life', his name is Christian and I met him in a church.

This practice is my soul sanctuary, a place to play, to explore, to process and to reconnect with Imogen and my higher self in the silver desert of stillness. I remain eternally grateful to the creator of this practice, Mother Raven, Gabrielle Roth, for this simple practice that has had an extraordinary effect on how I continue to dance through life. I bow in deep gratitude to your ever present spirit.

I watch as the flame from the tea light candle splutters and extinguishes itself in the pool of melted wax as I finish writing this chapter.

My body is still aching from the weekend's discovery of my soul power. I feel truly alive.

She's Back! The Return of Jezebel.

One of the first things I did when my ex-husband moved out was to redecorate my home. As our home was a two-bed flat, I moved into the living room, so my daughters could have a room each.

As Imogen moved into adolescence, it was quite evident she needed her own space. I didn't mind sleeping on a futon in the living room, or maybe I did, but I hadn't yet learned to honour my needs.

I painted the back wall of the living room turquoise with random large polka dots in various shades of pink. It made me happy. I then tackled the dull cement rendered fire- place, covering it in a swirling mosaic pattern of turquoise and orange glass tesserae. I could feel the blood flowing back into my being as I experienced being able to make my own choices about my living space without asking for consent or compromising what I desired. As a woman in her mid-thirties, it was long overdue. No wonder I had previously lost my identity. I could feel my previous sense of self gradually coming back to life, as I bought colour and creativity back into my environment. I dyed my mousy brown hair shocking pink, laughing at how 'normal' I appeared in my reflection in my own eyes.

Along with this rebirth of self, before the big sleep of my marriage years, I started to feel a stirring of a long forgotten feeling.

Was that my libido returning? Oh yes, it was!

For the final six years of my marriage, I had struggled with feeling any sexual feelings. This numbness had become such a concern for me that I had taken myself off to the GP who had run various blood tests on me. I was convinced my hormones must have been out of balance, or perhaps my thyroid was not working properly?

I had turned to the Internet in desperation to find out what was going on with me, as I understood my identity to be that of a highly libidinous creature. It would always be me with the higher sex drive in all of my relationships. So finding myself with no sexual feelings whatsoever, left me feeling like a stranger to myself.

I had written in various forums and online groups asking strangers for answers and advice, (somehow that was easier than talking to anyone close to me, it felt shameful, a failing). The Internet had decided almost unanimously that I was depressed. This was decidedly NOT the answer I was looking for.

I pushed back against these suggestions, saying that they'd misunderstood, that I loved my husband, it was clearly a chemical imbalance. (Oh how we can delude ourselves).

The doctor looked at the test results.
" Mrs Goldie, your bloods are entirely normal. There's nothing chemically amiss here but could I refer you for sex therapy sessions?"
I could feel my very normal blood start to boil. Didn't she understand? I knew how to do sex! I was a bloody expert at it! For fucks' sake!

I was livid, but on the outside I meekly responded, "No thanks, I'll be fine. Thanks for the information."

It wouldn't be more than a month later that I would ask the husband for a divorce.

Denial is a force to be reckoned with.

What I hadn't contended with, however, was that along with the return of my libido, I'd also return to Jezebel.

I realise now that this is who I thought I was, I had identified my adult sexual self with the acting out behaviour of a damaged child, a recipe for absolute catastrophe.

Dancing would become my way of dealing with all of this. There were all sorts of feelings that started to bubble up, thick, and fast. I found myself in clubs around London dancing to jazz, hip-hop and soulful house. The rhythm gave me a place to express myself and emptied my head of all the noise. I didn't drink, mostly as the music was all I needed to soothe me and let my expressive self shine.

Along with nightclubs, unfortunately for Jezebel, came predatory men. I would become entangled with one lecherous man after another, especially at the end of the night. These encounters would lead me into all sorts of dangerous and toxic situations. I realise now, at the time, I was slowly losing my mind, culminating in a psychotic break a year or so later.

All manner of dark energy forces seemed to sniff me out, and I found myself back in those dark, dangerous spaces that I was in back in my teenage years, except this time I was now a mum.

I tried to keep these encounters separate from the girls, mostly when they were at their dad's for the weekend, but as I lost my grip on reality, the boundaries started to blur.

It is this part of the story that I hold the deepest shame over. I know there were some awful situations that my acting out behaviours caused my daughters to be exposed to, and for that, I am deeply sorry. I know that had I had the opportunity to work through my childhood trauma before being a mum, maybe this wouldn't have happened. But life is messy, so all I can do is take accountability now that my inner child feels safe and heard.

Around about this time, I ended up being in an abusive relationship with a man who wouldn't leave me alone. He followed me home one night after a night out dancing and in my broken brain state, I figured that if I gave him what he wanted (head) he'd leave me alone.

Of course, he didn't and somehow his persistence and my complete lack of boundaries meant he moved in and became my boyfriend. I didn't even fancy him.

It's not difficult to spot the pattern at this point.

I would go on to have a complete nervous breakdown in this relationship after failed multiple attempts at getting him to leave, resulting in him violently raping me to break my resolve each time. Then he would shed crocodile tears on the doorstep if I actually managed to stay strong enough to follow through, and I'd relent, and the cycle would go round again.

I found myself naked in the street outside my home, talking to the trees and hiding from the cars because the cars were monsters. I have no recollection of how that night ended. I was just lucky not to be sectioned under the mental health act. No one knew I was so broken as the school run routine helped me mask my troubles and no one witnessed goings-on behind closed doors.

During this time, I'd had countless knives held to my throat. Walls and doors had holes punched in them, as well as knife marks from abusers stabbing through my doors. My entire flat was completely redecorated with a staple gun and his photos while I was out cold in a flu induced fever dream for two days.

I can't imagine how my girls must've felt during this time.

Imogen, by this point, had a lovely, stable, and steady boyfriend who she would visit. It would be three years before I could finally rid our home of this abuser.

One fateful night, he did the wrong thing. He broke my nose after a terrifying trip out to the West End. He was acting erratically and threateningly all night, threatening me with bottles and shouting in my face. When we got near my flat, I told him that he was not to come back. That he was to find somewhere else to live.

His response was dramatic. He punched me square in my face, breaking both my glasses and my nose, the sharp broken pieces of my glasses cutting into my face.

I ran straight to Brixton police station.

When I got there to report the assault, he was already there, pressing assault charges against me? It was quite obvious, by the bloody mess that was my face, who the victim was in this set of circumstances. He went to court on assault charges, during which time his female solicitor pulled me aside and begged me never to let him near me again.

Hitting me was a mistake for him as it woke me from the coercive control spell. It was clear to me that if someone hits you, they don't like you, let alone love you. The other stuff wasn't as clear for me but blood spilling out of my face was evidence I couldn't deny. This man was trouble. He would continue to harass me by driving slowly around my area for months after. I would find my body breaking into a panicked run every time I saw his car creeping along the kerb and him staring at me from behind the wheel.

That was difficult to write. I feel the full burden of guilt on my shoulders. I had wanted to be the best mum, but I had become the worst mum, a dangerous mum. I know that my acting out behaviours put my girls at risk and in situations that they really shouldn't have been in. Compulsion is painful to write about when you are through to the other side, when you aren't in the moment, with the invisible driving forces pushing you towards danger. It's so difficult to offer compassion to your broken past self. Because I was a mum, I should've been able to rise above these awful behaviours and put my children first. I know there will be people reading this judging me. I'm the first in the queue to judge myself, believe me. The person I've become finds it hard to reconcile with the person I once was. It was a tense few years of chaos where I also discovered my divided self.

55

My Divided Self Emerges

*I celebrate my unity with all life,
knowing we are all one.*

It's early on a Sunday morning. After a week of feeling frozen and stuck, I've woken up with a new perspective of potential.

Finally, things feel possible again.

Even if this feeling is set against what appears to be the rise of Fascism in the world at large, I've chosen to stay in my bubble. I do what I can to my best ability, to support myself and those around me to move away from a fear state, which I suspect has had something to do with my week of stuckness.

I know that meditation really helps me to centre myself, so I randomly decided to pick a short meditation from my phone with my intention of supporting my writing about the time of experiencing my divided self.

After the ten-minute communion with my higher self, I bemusedly noted that the randomly selected meditation's intention was about unity.

I pulled three tarot cards in a focus and gifts spread, the focus card being Temperance: balance, patience and unifying the spiritual and physical aspects. There appears to be a clear message pushing through here. These small synchronicities are like little breadcrumb rewards helping me find my way through difficult times, reminding me of my protection and guidance from unseen but certainly much felt energies.

During some of my earlier years of struggle, I wasn't aware of this guidance. I was solely focused on the physical world and I believed that everything that was happening, was happening TO me rather than FOR me. I experienced challenges as a punishment, consequence, or retribution rather than an opportunity to explore a wound brought to the surface or befriend a shadow that was brought into light.

It was during such a time when I found myself sunken into my deepest trauma and shame that they turned up to guide and protect me, the Baby and the Warrior.

Both characters were a manifestation of my unhealed pain. The baby was my vulnerability and clear personification of my inner child, sensitive, innocent, helpless, whereas the Warrior was the opposite, fearless yet numb, viciously sexual, predatory even, but mostly deeply protective of the Baby.

During times of high stress with any male partner, I would find myself flip-flopping between these two characters. It was not something I could control, as it seemed to happen as a triggered response to fear.

Warrior was personified fight, Baby was personified fawn and freeze. Once I'd shifted into either of these characters, I felt safe. Baby, despite being the completely unmasked self, embodying pure vulnerability, had a way of unsettling any potential abuser. Any potential aggressor would be so disturbed to see this change in me, it would snap them out of their focus, bringing them into a state of confusion. They would then almost be guaranteed to leave me alone.

If that didn't work, Warrior would rear into action in her fearless, numbed state and use physical aggression or aggressive sexuality to keep Baby safe. I never sensed any loss of time, and I was always conscious of my actions, so I don't think this would count as an alter, stemming from Dissociative Identity Disorder, as I wasn't dissociated, just split. I had witnessed sudden similar behavioural shifts in my mother as a small child, perhaps I had learned this from her as part of my 'normal'? Who knows?

Baby and Warrior would only appear in times of extreme distress, luckily they would be short-lived as the man I knew as Angel would help me to amalgamate both into one.

He did this very simply by observing my behaviour and calmly telling me to stop it, that he didn't believe it and most importantly, that I was safe and had no need to do it. That moment I'll never forget. By not feeding into the projection of these split characters, they simply dissolved into one another.

I think the technical term is integration. Whatever happened, it worked, and I've never experienced this split since. Maybe because during my time with Angel, I felt safe to crack open my Pandora's Box of hidden pain and start to make friends with the shadows and monsters lurking inside.

I remain deeply grateful to him.

I celebrate my unity with all life, I know I am all one. We are all one.

56

Sacred & Profane

Manifesting an Angel, Mother Monster and My Queen of Cups

I've not always been aware of my ability to create and craft my reality. It sort of crept up on me like a surprise party. Before the events of the past impactful decade, I felt as if the world's circumstances were moulding my everyday experiences, and I was just passively adapting to their most times negative forces. Life became about firefighting, never having enough time to feel safe in my surroundings, let alone, enjoy the view. But then death and birth turned up many times and shifted everything within a decade. In between the ages of 42 and 52, I lost my stepdad, Hennie, to suicide. A year and a half later, mum would die of bowel cancer at 65. The following year, Allegra would give birth to my first grandchild, Erykah. Three years later, my dear daddy died of COPD. Two years later, my grandson Olly was born and then at the end of the following year, 2016, Imogen and her husband Rob decided life was too much for them.

Hennie's brief and tragic suicide note to my mum read,

" Darling, I could not live up to your expectations. H x "

My outwardly stern but inwardly kind stepdad, who was in his mid-eighties, had hanged himself in his garage after coming through a series of strokes that had left him mostly deaf and with tunnel vision. My mum being twenty years his junior and also a tricky person to please, (to put it kindly) must have made Hennie's disabilities feel quite overwhelming. I was not surprised by what he did. The news of my mother's bowel cancer diagnosis came via text after I'd severed all ties with her, going no-contact after we'd had an enormous fight a few years earlier during her visit to London in my early 40s.

Throughout my life I'd always managed to excuse my mother's often erratic, most times emotionally wounding behaviour to myself and others by deftly finding the reason underlying that particular outburst to make it either forgivable, palatable or understandable, (preferably all three). I called this 'finding wiggle room'. I realise now that this coping behaviour, rooted in my inner child's need to keep herself safe, had created my special interest in human psychology.

This understanding also helped me mask in neurotypical society as learning the rules and performing was key to hiding your lack of understanding of them. This led to my authentic self not being seen by others or ultimately by myself.

My mother had always been quite openly racist in her attitude, but would strongly deny that she was if challenged. She confused her fetishisation of black men's bodies with anti-racism, (I grew up with many a poster of Mohammed Ali on the walls at home). It was clear that she was comfortable with and ignorant to her deeply ingrained belief of white supremacy. This was evident by the way she wholeheartedly embraced the white privilege that came with being an English im- migrant to apartheid South Africa. She left England as a working-class woman and entered Cape Town as a middle-class woman by sheer virtue of her white skin.

Then one day I would stare her racism dead in the face and desperately try to find the wiggle room.

In the midst of my nervous breakdown years, I took my girls to visit their grand- parents in South Africa. They had retired to a tiny 'dorpie' called VanWyksdorp near Ladysmith in the Western Cape.

Imagine driving along a mountain pass in the countryside, turning off into a dirt road, then following that dirt road for miles and miles until it stops. That was how remote my parents' village was. There were vineyards, ostriches, a church, one shop, a police station with a single jail cell and a post office that served a tiny population of around 600 people, mostly farm workers. The annual donkey derby was the cultural highlight of the year. The rumour was, that the farm workers would be paid in wine on a Friday night. The village police officer would drive around in his truck, picking up the drunk workers and lock them up in the single cell for the night to sleep off the effects of the wine.

Mum lived in a handsome white house in the village, with an outdoor spring and a large garden.

She had prepared places for us all to sleep. Imogen had her bed in the study, while Allegra and I were to share a double bed in the guest room.

The first morning, I woke up after a fitful nights sleep and I felt strangely damp. I turned to ten year old Allegra, accusing her of wetting the bed. She pointed at me and said,
" No, mum, it was you. "
To my absolute horror, I discovered she was right.

When I told my mum, shamefacedly, what had happened, she seemed remarkably upbeat about it all, happy almost? I was expecting rage and I got... satisfaction? Was that the feeling I was picking up?

My body was showing me just how terrified I was about this whole experience.

The rest of the trip was a mixture of happy memories of my girls in the South African countryside and the contrast of constantly walking on eggshells around my mum. Imogen was shouted at more than a few times by mum for slamming doors when she just couldn't contain her frustration any longer. The trip wasn't fun for her or for me.

I was so relieved when I returned home. I would be paying off that trip on my credit card for years after.

I was just glad I'd ticked that duty box.

I realised looking back that I'd inadvertently manifested an Angel of a man who would enter my life and soothe my soul.

Not long after the nose breaking incident, my lovely friend Lena gave me a thin paper-back book with the disclaimer of "I'm not usually into this Californian New Age stuff, but it's worth a go!"

The book was a step-by-step guide to manifesting what you truly deserved and desired by uncovering deep subconscious blocks and negative self talk by a process of automatic writing. It took pages and pages of writing to quieten my inner imposter who seemed determined I didn't deserve what I was asking for, but I finally managed it.

I'd asked for someone in my life who was kind.

It was a simple and heartfelt request that reflected just how unkind my environment must have felt at that time. I'd concurrently been collecting anything to do with angels, figurines, books, cards, stickers, anything that caught my eye, and I'd also painted Mary Magdalene surrounded by angels and putti on my kitchen ceiling, Michelangelo style.

It felt good and safe to be surrounded by angels. It was only in hindsight, after being in a relationship with this kind young man called Angel (his nickname that had stuck) that I made the connection.

At 40 years old, I had met and fallen in love with a much younger man called Angel. He was 25 but had a deeply serious and mature side, with a silly soft core that reminded me fondly of my dad. We met online and spoke via Messenger for six months before meeting, doing the teenage crush thing of falling asleep on the phone to one another. We would go on to become lovers, best friends and life partners for 13 beautiful years.

This would go down as the relationship that transformed my life for the better, him being my confrontational mirror, my unconditional source of love, my rock, my safety blanket.

I felt loved to my core, deep into my bone marrow.

We shared a common strong sense of justice, we both spoke for hours about Patriarchy and its impact on society for me as a woman, and for him as a black man of Jamaican origin.

This would be the easiest relationship of my life, there was no need for drama or game playing. We could talk through our differences and occasional misunderstandings.

For the first time, I was with a man who saw me for who I was in entirety, not for my body parts or what he could get from me, but for how he connected with my soul. If grief hadn't blown us apart dramatically when it did, I'm sure we would still be together, cosy, and habitual.

The Universe, however, had other ideas, possibly because during our time together, I had shifted form from Mother to Enchantress, and I was heading towards Crone. This age gap was starting to feel pointed as spiritually the gulf started to grow between us when my entire being shifted into a new incarnation. Spirit suddenly became all important to me and I lost him on an esoteric level, as I entered a new and surrendered part of my life. It was a damn shame that he was sacrificed as part of my letting go process. I still deeply love him to this day.

When we were still together, Angel had agreed to meet my mother at the airport when she came on a rare visit from South Africa. I couldn't go as I had inescapable work commitments, so he stepped up in my place.

Mother was greeted warmly with his big smile and impeccable manners, I was very proud of my partner, he was an impressive, kind human being. Knowing that my mother was a complex character (and racist) the courage and kindness he showed her for my benefit was something quite remarkable.

Mum stayed in our bedroom for the duration of her visit. We slept in the living room on a futon.

One afternoon, Angel was out at work and mum and I were in the kitchen catching up after her trip up to Scotland to see my sister and her partner. Allegra was in her bedroom. Imogen had made herself scarce during her grandma's stay, she wasn't fond of her energy. Mum stood in the kitchen doorway next to Allegra's bedroom while I washed the dishes at the kitchen sink. The conversation centred around my sister and her new boyfriend. Mum expressed how much she liked my sister's new boyfriend. I fed back that I wasn't so sure what to think of him as some things my sister had told me about him weren't conducive to an ideal relationship. I didn't expect this comment to trigger her next response:

"Well, Diane, in an IDEAL world your partner wouldn't be young and black, now would he?"

The wiggling started.
Young? Well, that she could have. Ageism I would tolerate. That was probably rooted in jealousy, after all she had said how attractive she thought he was (a very uncomfortable moment).
Black? What was her issue there?
My brain whirred, wildly searching through all its available files for the wiggle room. Why would she say that? What other reason apart from racism would explain this comment?
No, there it was.
The inescapable truth, my mum was a racist.

I exploded in a rage of logical patterned words, "Would you rather me be with a white man who did (this) to me?

Or this black man who wakes up to check I'm okay every time I go to the toilet in the middle of the night? Or what about these white men who did (this) and (this) to me? Was that ideal?"

I reeled off a litany of sins visited on my body by white men in my past, clearly Jezebel was levelling up to become Medusa.

My rage grew to the point where I grabbed a knife on the draining board and stepped towards my source of pain.

Luckily, Allegra had heard the commotion and came running in to the kitchen, knocked the knife out of my hand and hugged me tightly, rocking me back and forth.

My mother walked calmly into my (her) bedroom and didn't come out for the next two days.

I can look back now and understand this moment as a meltdown triggered by years of built-up childhood trauma that exploded all at once in a violent release. This would be a defining moment that I would come to recognise (al- beit not acceptable to threaten your mother with a knife) that my raging inner child had finally stood up for herself and said no more.
I had slain the Mummy Monster, Mummy had no power over me any longer.

Mum could be highly sexually inappropriate with her grandchildren too. Before this stand-off, she had commented to Allegra and me that we were lucky because we had (an arm gesture indicating a large erection) and sadly, she was stuck with (wiggles her baby finger). This was another racially charged comment, as both Allegra and I were in relationships with men of Jamaican heritage at the time. Such weird, cringe worthy and highly offensive behaviour, what was Mum thinking?

After the kitchen explosion, Mum still hadn't finished with me. She waited until Angel finished work, then, utilising his peacemaker energy, she invited him into her place of self-exile (our bedroom) and embarked on a six-hour attempt at total character annihilation of my being. This culminated in her saying I was still in love with my ex-husband, and I was possibly cheating on him with my ex. Oh, and that he'd better go back and see me, as I would be jealous of him giving her so much attention.

What mum hadn't factored in to this foul plan was our couple's superpower of open and honest communication. Once mum said I was in love with my ex-husband still, he knew everything was a lie.

Afterwards, as he reported back to me, word for bitter word of the litany of lies and hate infused barbs that my own mother had thrown at me, he hugged me tightly and whispered,

"Your strength is remarkable. When you said she was difficult, I had no idea you were dealing with this level of trauma."

This felt so safe, and I felt so seen, understood and completely supported.

One important thing I knew was, it was time to go no-contact with my mother. She had not only proven that she didn't love me, but that she was actively trying her best to harm me.

She had flipped my switch.

The next day, I walked into her room and calmly asked her to pack her bags and leave because she was no longer welcome in my home. She then said, puzzlingly that she was going to go down to the police station to report me? Report me for what exactly, mum? I reminded my mother that here in the UK, it wasn't a crime to disagree with your parents especially now I was an adult. What a very strange attempt at a threat. She was a guest in my home and now her welcome had come to an end. I ordered her a cab and took my dog out for a long walk in the driving rain, rather than having to face the final, inevitable barb that would come with goodbye.

My daughters told me she had taken it out on them instead.

Six months later, I received a text from her telling me that she had three months to live. Turns out that sudden weight loss that she had celebrated was terminal bowel cancer, and she had been sent home with morphine. Her current partner of two months would be caring for her. His name was Reuben, and she had met him online. He had moved in with her almost immediately.

One evening a few months later, I got a long-distance call from mum. She was high as a kite on morphine, waxing lyrically about the moon. She went on to say she had signed her estate over to Reuben, the boyfriend, so that he could take care of selling the house after she was gone and split the money between my sister and me.

I knew immediately that mum had been scammed by this Lothario. I told mum I had no interest in her money and that I doubted very much that Reuben would do what she'd asked of him. I knew that once she was dead, he'd be off with her money, never to be seen again.

Then she insisted that I tell her I loved her,
"Tell me you love me, Diane!"
I was still so angry with her.
"I can say words, but I can't back them up with feeling, mum".
"Just say it!"
"I love you"
"Say it again!"

"I love you, mum."
The following morning I received a text from Reuben confirming that mum had died in the night.

That same night, my lovely epileptic dog had eight fits, one after the other. I had him put to sleep the next day.

Reuben disappeared just as I thought he might, with the deeds of mums house and everything she'd ever owned. I felt sad for my sister, as she'd lost both parents plus any memorabilia or inheritance due to her because of mum's complicated ways and vulnerability to the charms of scheming con-men.

I may sound cold when I say this, but mum's death came as a relief to me. Gone were the constant mind games and emotional manipulations. It felt like I could breathe once more.

Another prediction would soon manifest. Years earlier, I had been given a tarot reading that was very peculiarly precise. The reader had said that in my midlife, I'd meet a white haired, eccentric older woman who would change my life and set me on my true path. She was represented by the Queen of Cups. Fast-forward into my mid-forties, I'd created a hand-painted tote bag featuring Caravaggio's Medusa on the front, one of my favourite paintings. I uploaded a photo of it to Facebook, and it was immediately bought by a former New Yorker outsider artist named Sue Kreitzman, who lived in London's East End. A colourful, eccentric older lady, with, yes, you guessed it, white hair.

Here she was, my Queen of Cups.
Sue would go on to champion me and replace my mother's toxic earworm of " You'll never be an artist " with "You're an artistic genius."

I would go on to create kimonos for Sue that turned her into her own walking art gallery, utilising my copying skills to translate Sue's own distinct artwork into fabric through hand painting and appliqué.

As I learned my craft as I went on, I began to develop my own particular visual style. I would go on to dress Grammy award-winning musical legends like Jill Scott, Jacob Collier and Tank and the Bangas, to name a few. My whole world shifted through the loving gaze and recognition of this Queen of Hearts and Cups. Her words of encouragement drowned out my own inner saboteur. Thank you, Sue, your mentorship and love has been invaluable and profound.

57

Reflections of Me

When it comes to friendships, I've always struggled to find the right person. It seemed to me, especially as a young person, that I always gravitated towards the wrong people. Until the nuns guided me to the uncomplicated and true friendship with Cara, my scarecrow, I had found retaining friendships difficult. This was confusing to me because once I am your friend, I will be loyal, honest, and generous to a fault. You will know every last corner of my soul if you are prepared to listen to my stories and obviously, I'll love to listen to yours. I'll cook for you, play you my favourite music, share with you my favourite art, films and plays, I'll be silly and selfless. Don't expect me to be constantly checking in on you, though. I'll presume you realise we both have busy lives and that we are always in one another's thoughts. I know that if you need me, you will reach out, and I'll do the same, and when you do, I will drop everything to be by your side. Once we are back in each other's company, it will be like no time has passed. That could be a few days or even a few years, you will feel like home to me. There will be no resentment nor awkwardness and no need to fill in the gaps where insecurity lies because we have one another's back forever. Forever, that is, unless you break my trust. Then I will never pay attention to you again, it will be like you never existed. The switch is either on or off. I've come to understand this comes from my need to be totally open in a relationship, this openness requires vulnerability and deep trust to feel safe. Violate the boundary of trust and I have to excommunicate you from my life because now I feel exposed and scared, wondering if I ever really knew you at all? Was it all an illusion? What were your intentions with me?

Having to keep an open heart to experience intimacy has its risks and with risk, sometimes you win, sometimes you lose.

Lovely Lena, my Swedish support system

One of my most long-lasting and ongoing friendships has been with lovely Lena, a Swedish mum around my age who I first met in our children's primary school play- ground. Like me, she also had two beautiful daughters who were three years apart in age, hers being just one year older than my girls. We quickly discovered we had a lot in common, we had both worked in catering before having children, both shared a common interest in art and language. Despite being dyslexic, and English being her second language, Lena had a degree in English Literature from Gold- smiths that I found incredibly impressive as she had managed somewhat miracu- lously to complete it while her children were young. She was also a poet, writing about domesticity and the female landscape. I found her poems very moving and thought-provoking. Above all, Lena shared my silly, which was the ultimate personal attribute for me. A lightness of spirit seemed a guarantee of 'good folk' that helped my body to understand that this person could be trusted. Like the Dowlings at the Green House back in South Africa, Lena gave me a safe feeling of home, of comfort and warmth, she was easy to be friends with. She introduced me to Swedish culture, midsummer ritual and song, which delighted my inner child immensely. Wearing flower crowns and dancing in a ring, making various animal noise impressions, was just up my street!

My girls also became ready friends with hers and all four girls would play together, making up dance routines and eating fresh mulberries from the tree in the back garden, having an idyllic, innocent time together. For a while, Lena's youngest, Greta, a talented percussionist and now avant-garde composer, would be Imogen's first drummer in her musical adventures. Greta's creative style of jazzy rhythm perfectly complimented Imogen's quirky, grungy, soulful rock songs.

One of Imogen's earliest and most beautiful songs was called Bjerke. It was a song written about Lena's family Swedish summerhouse that was nestled in the beautiful Swedish countryside.

Bjerke

(Written when Imogen was 17, this song speaks in haiku'esque lyrics about her love for Lena's Swedish Summer house)

The guitar accompaniment to this song is so complex that many of my accomplished musician friends find it challenging to play.

Calm down, take it easy
This house is busy
Take me back to
Where I don't want to leave you , leave you

Bjerke, a part of me
Lobacken and everything beyond
Built around a fountain of life
In certainty, lie down in feathers
Take in the Swedish weather.

We have been lucky enough to be invited there a couple of times to experience this domestic, simple, basic, perfect, heaven on earth place. With its ornate cast iron wood burning stove, who's belly you fed with logs to create the heat to cook the pancakes, outdoor decorated long drop double seated toilet, loom in the bedroom, open fires, old lace and family portraits lovingly painted, ticking clocks, rag rugs, washing in the pantry, eating what was there, ice cold showers on the porch, unique lifestyle. It was so far removed from our inner city South London flat life that it was tantamount to being on another planet. Entertainment was a home made zip wire in the trees, finding bugs or Chanterelle mushrooms in the nearby forest, chopping logs to feed the open fires and the beautiful stove, making fairy rings in the long grass, sitting quietly, taking in the sun under the bunting on the porch with a big mug of coffee, bike rides down long country lanes and swimming in cold, clear and deserted fresh water lakes where the sand sparkled under the bronze water, like gold glitter.

After my divorce, when Lena saw how chaotic I'd become, she invited me and my girls out to the Summer house for an opportunity to 'fall apart in her backyard'.

This beautiful gesture of kindness I shall always treasure, alongside her slipping me her backdoor key to her home, just in case I ever needed to run somewhere safe. That is true sisterhood in action. She supported me through my messiest of times and I hope I've been there for her too when she's needed me.

After Imogen's death we would return to the heaven on earth that was Lena's Summer house to film a part of a short documentary about

Imogen's life. Lena, always the most delightful host, welcomed the tiny film crew into her Swedish sanctuary so we could try to recreate and honour some of Imogen's favourite memories there.

Some of our most memorable times together were when Lena joined me in my children's entertainment venture, becoming my driver and very capable sidekick, 'Aunty Lena'. Drawing from Swedish culture, her outfit reflected the blue Swedish summer sky and a nod to flower crowns, with her straw hat bedecked with flowers and blue cotton dress painted with butterflies. She was a perfect compliment to my outfit of sparkles and ribbons, reflecting my Romany heritage. We made quite the eccentric pair. London's under five party scene embraced us wholeheartedly, and we were a popular and busy pair of silly ladies for almost a decade. Lena wrote stories for my puppet shows and fell in love with my piggy policeman puppet PC Porker with his no-nonsense but kind ways. He was her kind of guy.

Lena also had a strange physical reaction to tall, well-built men, going literally weak at the knees in their presence. I'd never encountered such an extreme physical response before, and it tickled my silly bone immensely.

When we were booked to entertain for a party for the family of England's Rugby captain, Lawrence Dallaglio, I knew we were in trouble.

By this point, Lena had become a proficient and delicate face painter, despite her initial reluctance towards this skill. When Mr Dallaglio himself sat down opposite Lena and asked to be painted as Spider-Man, I knew I had to rescue her before she collapsed in a dramatic Jane Austin style faint.

Then there was the time at a posh mummy's party where a pretty little girl, no more than 4 years of age, asked Aunty Lena to face-paint her as a rocket. It started off well enough, but grew increasingly dubious as Lena started to panic as she had to recall what an actual rocket looked like. This was before the time of smartphones, there was no way of checking with a quick Google search. Any image would have to rely on recall. The rocket developed a triangular mushroom style tip. It was at the point of her deciding to include some engines at the base of the rocket that I looked over to discover that Aunty Lena had managed to paint what looked very much like a crude erect penis on this four-year-old, innocent girl's face. Of course, this was completely inadvertently done. As soon as I'd stopped giggling at the outrageous circumstance we found ourselves in, I stepped into Aunty Lena's place to fix this phallic faux pas, and to reassure this precious child that her rocket was going to be the best rocket ever. How we managed to fix this without anyone seeing what we had almost done was beyond me. The relief we felt soon fuelled our giggly hysteria, we barely managed to hold it together to the end of the party without collapsing into fits of giggles. We had to avoid looking at one another. So close, we were so close to becoming the next clown sex offender headline in the Daily Mail.

Sakli and the journey to making the film

The mystery of meeting my Queen of Cups, Sue Kreitzman, would be the next link in the chain leading me to meeting one of the most important, powerful and influential people in my life. When I first met her, she was called Laurence, or Lolo to those in her inner circle. Now her name is Sakli, received through a significant ancestral journey in her life.

But first, let me tell you how Spirit threw me at her. I look back with astonishment at how this occurred.

I had been creating wearable art kimonos for Sue, and she had been invited to exhibit them and her sculptures and neck shrines in an East End shop called Cult Mountain. At this point of my journey I was still a fledgling creative, very socially awkward, uncomfortable in my skin and in public settings where I could be perceived, especially exhibition openings where mingling and small talk was required. I pushed myself to go, however, as I wanted to support Sue and also show up for myself. My 4-year-old granddaughter was with me as she really loved Sue and the weird art people around her. I'd managed to step out of my jeans and tee-shirt uni- form (mask) and I had customised a purple velvet coat with an image of Medusa on the back for the event. Once I was there I found myself hiding in corners awkwardly with my granddaughter, reluctant to mingle with anyone. I just found it all too difficult.

Then I saw her.

The most beautiful woman I'd ever seen walked into the exhibition. She wore her locced hair up with the undercut visible, her elegant neck with tattoos and scarification etched onto her dark skin. She was dressed in loose, flowing, elegant garments and her hair was topped off with a hat that would make Erykah Badu envious. When she turned around, she had the most beautiful face, like a cross between Eartha Kitt and Brenda Fassie and a gorgeous gap-toothed smile that suggested a wicked sense of fun. I was transfixed, hypnotised, and slightly intimidated. Something made me break out of my trance and I stumbled over to her, awkwardly mumbling the words:
"I need to know you".
It felt like spirit had shoved me in my back, whispering loudly in my ear:

IT'S HER! GO ON!

We met for lunch the following week after I had created a short cape for her in- spired by her body art. This would be my first personal storytelling piece that set the style for my wearable art for the next ten years, setting the aesthetic that would go on to be recognised globally. Sakli would go on to become my 'wifey', not in any sexual sense as both of us were reluctant heterosexuals, but would treat one another with the same amount of care and trust as any romantic partner. Every so often, we would joke that we wished our significant others had treated us the way we treated one another. Both being Taureans, we understood that we were sensual and stubborn creatures, and we understood how to honour one another's spirit through all five senses. Sakli is a gifted aromatherapist and bodyworker, a healer working with direct support and communication with the ancestors. To describe her simply as a masseur is doing her a deep disservice. She has held me during the process of writing this book, her spirit and healing hands have been deeply appreciated. It's difficult to describe our relationship with words, all I know is that we are a visual defiance to Patriarchy. Our bond is deep, secure, and quiet. I feel safe, seen and truly loved in her presence. Our friendship is embodied hope for a better world where differences are celebrated and similarities honoured. A world where disagreements can be held and respected without the ego insisting on being right, where one another's vulnerabilities are cherished and protected. I deeply love this woman.

It would be Sakli who would put me forward to be interviewed by US mother and daughter vlogging team StyleLikeU, where I would end up stripping off layers of clothing, sitting on a stool, whilst sharing increasingly vulnerable aspects of my life's journey. This video would go viral and reach the eyes of a special human, film-maker, director Alma Hare'l who left a comment that she would love to give me a hug. A year later, I would find myself in New York, courtesy of the kindness of my Queen of Cups, Sue Kreitzman who had invited me out to visit her USA home. The timing was such that I was able to attend the opening night of Alma's documentary film Love True at the Tribeca Film Festival. The Universe seemed to be lining things up for me. I was seated next to Alma's closest friend Margo as we watched this extraordinary poetic and artistic documentary about love unfold. Alma got her hug and at the same screening there would be a young fan of Alma's called Lola who would become the co-director of our beautiful short documentary of Imogen's life.

Photo of Imogen used in the film

Margo, who I was seated next to in the screening, would be our producer (what a woman!) and Alma would be our executive producer. The making of this intense 30 minute documentary would turn out to be an experience we'd never forget, mirror- ing Imogen's intense short life. The tiny crew consisted of two co-directors, one who doubled up as a sound person, a cinematographer, and two key actors who would immerse themselves in Imogen's story, playing Imogen and Rob. The filming was done in a Gestalt fashion, completely in the moment, there was no rehearsal or script. Every key scene in Imogen's life was recreated, the actors immersed them- selves in their characters, and Allegra and I played ourselves. Every scene was shot in one take. We returned to Lena's Swedish summer house to film interviews in Imogen's favourite place. Her journals, written over a period of 17 years, would form the key driver of her story as we were keen for Imogen's authentic voice to be heard in the retelling of her struggles. The whole process was a strange and in- tense process of active grieving, as we were forced to confront our pain on camera.

Imogen herself was the motivation for making this film. She had left behind clear instructions in her lyric book that I was to take her music to the world. This had proven to be a rather difficult challenge, as all of Imogen's later music had described her journey through heroin addiction. What mother would feel comfortable releasing this music into the world without providing context, without first giving her baby back her humanity?

We worked very closely with the Samaritans to make sure our film would do no harm but at the same time, I was keen to be open and honest about Imogen's drug use. I was very aware that shame was at the very core of her inability to tell any of her family or friends about her struggles with addiction. It was shame that gave her no way out and kept her trapped. I wanted to do everything in my power to lift that stigma and start an open conversation around self-medicating, especially in the context of people struggling with unsupported neurodivergence.

I strongly believe this forms a part of my joint mission that I know I'm on with Imogen. Our mission is to support, educate and identify by storytelling, those others like her who struggled to understand their own 'baby brains'.

There is a path through self judgement to self acceptance that can ease the way into a life that can better support your needs. Firstly, masks need to fall, once you start to realise that you are not a broken neurotypical but a perfectly normal neurodivergent, the path to self-love can begin.

I can personally attest to the power of this process as I have taken these steps myself and have experienced just how impactful making these changes can be. Sakli has been very much involved in helping me with this journey.

Understanding myself and my family through the neurodivergent lens (specifically AUDHD) has been the most validating process, as I've been able to unpack previously misunderstood behaviours and look upon our struggling selves with so much more compassion. There have been so many lightbulb moments as I look upon myself and my nearest and dearest through this new filter.

Unfortunately, a global pandemic interfered with the release plans for Imogen's film. Now it sits in a place of limbo online, but despite its lack of exposure, it still managed to win an anti-stigma award and be nominated for best short music film at the UKVMA's in 2021.

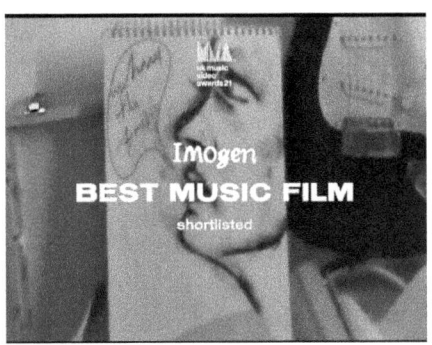

So Imogen, the world did go on to hear your music after all.

Without that initial push from spirit to collide into Sakli, none of this would have happened. The Universe has a clear plan with signposts, if you are prepared to let go of the oars of your boat and observe the river bank as you float gently down the stream.

What is ours will come to us, by hook or by crook, if we can let go of trying to force it to happen.

The Off-Switch is Activated.

Not all my friendships have been this mutually beneficial. I have had to learn the hard way, that my open and trusting heart can sometimes be taken advantage of. My boundaries have had to be strengthened to protect myself, my off-switch was soon to be activated once again.

I had recently got the news that Imogen had taken her life out in Cambodia. I had a few days to get myself together, raise funds and fly over to Phnom Penh to cremate her, bringing her ashes and what remained of her belongings back home. In my numb state, I set up a crowdfunder on social media, I was relying on the kindness of strangers to help me afford to do what I had to do. Within a day, the target had been reached and doubled. I was overwhelmed with gratitude and shocked at the outpouring of love and the generosity of people I barely knew. This was such a reminder that despite what the internet tells us, the human spirit is kind, especially in times of crisis. Because I had extra money at my disposal, I was able to bring along someone to support Allegra and me in our hour of need. One friend reached out to me saying she had experience of travelling in Cambodia and Thail- and as she and her twin sister had travelled there often. She was tall, strong and felt grounded, so I agreed to bring her with us as our support system.

It wasn't long before the alarm bells started to ring.

At the airport, I noticed that she hadn't changed up any currency. I thought perhaps she may have had US dollars with her from her previous travels, so I pushed it aside. I had pre-booked a two-bedroom hotel suite for us with prepaid breakfasts for everyone. I figured that even though we wouldn't be very hungry, it was sensible to start the difficult days off with something to fuel us. I had changed up a bunch of cash into US dollars (the preferred currency in Cambodia) to cover our incidental costs.

The day of the cremation arrived, and we all did what we had to do.

Afterwards, Allegra, who was understandably distressed, took some prescribed medication and went to lie down in the room that I shared with her.

The friend had a separate bedroom to herself in the suite. The friend, let's call her Lou, had brought her laptop with her as she said she wanted to catch up with some work while she was there. She was going through her messages and emails when she discovered that quite by chance, a friend, and her partner were in Phnom Penh just down the street from our hotel. She said she wanted to go out and meet her and I agreed, in my grief addled state I thought it was a coincidence so she should follow it up.

Now I look back, and can clearly see that this was all pre-planned from the start.

When we first entered the hotel suite, Lou had hugged me. As she held me tight she had muttered,

"How are you so strong?" over and over.

That confused me? What was she asking me? I wasn't strong, and I answered her as such,

"I'm not strong, I'm just doing what I have to do as a mum."

Of course, I was going to do my duty to my daughter and give her a dignified send-off.

Of course, I wanted to say goodbye to her.

It struck me how disappointed Imogen must have been that her father had decided not to come.

It was his prerogative, I suppose.

Someone had to hold things together for my other baby and grandchildren's sake, and that someone was me.

Lou asked me for some spending money so she could go out and see her friend. I gave her a few notes, she looked disappointed and asked for more. I obliged, maybe she knew more about prices as she'd been here before. I asked her to not stay out too late as we only had one key card, I would rather not have to wait up too long to let her in.

I was rudely awakened from my fitful slumbers at 3am by loud banging and drumming on the hotel door. Lou stumbled in, clearly very intoxicated, and started drumming loudly on all the wooden surfaces in the suite, the noise reverberating around the early morning quiet. I desperately tried to quieten her down, as I didn't want her to wake up Allegra or get complaints from other hotel guests. I made Lou eat some food I'd saved for her, trying to mop up excess intoxicants and calm her down. Then I asked her to go to bed.

I managed to get her into her bedroom, shut the door after her and crawled off, exhausted, overwhelmed and angry, to try to get some sleep of my own. Thankfully, Allegra was still sound asleep thanks to the medication.

Suddenly, my bedroom door burst open and Lou launched her tall, strong self on to my bed, landing with her full body-weight on top of mine. Winded, I went into shock as she pinned me down and started pulling at my pyjama top all the time muttering incoherent sentences, some bits I could make out sounded like,

"Leave him come be with me."

This scared me. She continued to lower her full body over mine, pulled up my pyjama top exposing my naked breast and bit me hard just next to the nipple, leaving a large purple welt, that would turn into a spectacular bruise that I would go home to show to my shocked partner.

Something in me snapped and I silently (because I was so aware of not wanting to wake Allegra to witness this traumatic scene unfolding on the worst night of all of our lives) roared and reared up with superhuman strength, pushing her off me, dragging her out of the room and back to her bed.

By some miracle, she calmed down and fell asleep.

In the morning, I pulled Allegra aside and told her what had transpired that previous night. We both decided we would ignore Lou from that moment on. It made for an extremely awkward long flight home, but Lou didn't deserve an ounce more of my precious energy. After we got home, she would go on to bombard me with texts and emails as if nothing had happened, asking me why I was ignoring her. She even turned up at my home unannounced, my partner answered the door, she barged past him to find me, hugged me, then spun around on her heel and left with no explanation, leaving as quickly as she'd arrived. I was left standing completely aghast, mouth open in shock. Later I would email her to explain exactly why I was ignoring her, that she had sexually assaulted me on the night I cremated my baby. She emailed me back a long email, furiously denying that her interaction that night was sexual assault. She claimed that she was just being playful, as she was with many of her friends.

How could it have been sexual assault when she had done the same thing to many of her friends and also to her mother?

This email left me reeling. She had confessed to assaulting her friends and her own mother and thought it was normal. She apologised for making me feel as if I had been sexually assaulted and asked, if circumstances had been different, would I have flagged this up as problematic at all?

The simple answer was yes. A million times, yes.

Sigh.

I later invited her around to give her the chance to apologise and take accountability for her actions. I knew that the likelihood of my bumping into her at social events was very high, given we had so many mutual friends.

She did apologise, but I've heard that she has continued with this behaviour with others. All I could do was protect myself, so the switch was flipped.

I look back at this shocking event that had heaped trauma upon trauma, and wondered if she was reflecting my extremely broken inner child back at me?

She felt like my Jezebel manifest who had come to me in a time of intense vulnerability when my boundaries were at their weakest. I would learn from then on to be far more discerning with my friendships and would build back up some strong boundaries again to protect my vulnerable spirit, enabling my heart to break open without fear in future.

Vincey

Portrait of my soul sun, Vince

If it hadn't been for Lou, however, I may never have met one of my most beautiful and radiant soul friends. For the introduction to Vince, I remain eternally grateful to her.

I first encountered this ray of sunshine at home in my living room. I was seated on a red swivel chair at the computer, back turned to the television. My partner was watching a new reality show that I had little interest in, called The Voice. Singers would try to get the judges to turn their red swivel chairs around by the power of the voice alone. Should the judges like what they heard, they pressed their " I want you" buzzers, and they would swivel around to see who was singing. I thought it was a bit gimmicky and paid it no mind. I focused on my computer screen until I heard a voice that made me turn around in my own, albeit much smaller office type red swivel chair, to see who was singing Madonna's Like a Virgin in such a soulful manner. This would be the first time I would see my darling Vincey. He would make it all the way through to the finals of the show before being pipped at the post by some other person that everyone has forgotten by now. By this point, I had become totally invested in Vince and had championed him all the way to the final, hoping he'd win. He certainly deserved to, in my opinion.

A few years later he would be knocking on my door, sent by Lou who he had briefly worked alongside, to see if he could borrow some stage wear from me. From the moment I opened the door and heard
"You alright, babes?"

I fell in pure platonic love with this enormous spirit with the prettiest face and nightingale voice. He has the most beautiful soul and the silly gene. That was the magic combination. Our bond was sealed that very first moment when he asked me for a hug. Vince was a New Year's Eve baby like Imogen, and I played her music to him, which he loved. At this point, Imogen was still with us, albeit really struggling. I told Imogen all about my meeting with Vince, she looked him up online, listened to some of his more commercial songs and declared, in typical unfiltered Imogen fashion:
"He's shit."
Imogen didn't mince her words and was a proud musical snob, rejecting any pop sensibility as commercial nonsense. I persevered and sent her his new, at the time unreleased music and she totally changed her attitude. The two of them struck up conversation and went on to form a firm, albeit brief, friendship and mutual respect.

When Imogen died, Vince was right there for me. He would sit with me, drink tequila together and dance with me, and we also spent time in the recording studio making music together. He wrote some beautiful tribute songs for her and me, one extraordinary song was called Shelter You, which was about trying to hold me through my grief. I'll never forget the moment that he played it to me for the first time. Hearing his soulful, pain infused vocals as the gospel infused track powered through intense emotion really penetrated my heart, releasing tears as I felt the resonance of his pure aligned intention. I leaned into the trust and was held in support, knowing I was safe to fall apart completely in his presence.

This friendship has always felt pure and uncomplicated, despite our clear generational age gap, our inner children found it easy to connect with one another. Silly was our shared language, dance, and music our playground. Vince also had a clear spiritual connection with Imogen that would make itself known on a few extraordinary occasions. One notable time, we'd got together to write some original songs. I'd brought along with me, Imogen's treasured lyric book, retrieved from Cambodia. Inside this small, leather-bound notebook were lyrics to all of her songs. Many songs had been recorded and stored on flash drives, but there was one song lyric that had not had a chance to have music added before she died. They were angry lyrics, that seemed to be directed towards her father. It felt important to complete this song for her, so Vince and I set out in this session to write a song all about Daddy issues.

Spirit, however, had other ideas.

As the song started to evolve, so did the tone and intention of the lyrics. We must've been connected with our higher selves because nothing negative was allowed to flow through. The intention of the song went from being angry to that of gratitude for the opportunity of evolving and growing our spirit through challenge.

I read Imogen's unfinished song lyrics over the musical outtro in one take with no rehearsal. Like magic, they fitted perfectly into the space left at the end of the song. The process of the song creation was seamless and felt inevitable.

As Vince finished laying down the vocals and left the room, he felt a kick in his back. No one was there. Imogen was very 'handy' with her feet when she got excited. She used to have regular foot fights with her sister, it was a 'thing' that was peculiar to her.

Vince read it straight away as her presence and acknowledgement of the magical process of creation of the song, Spirit Evolving.

As we later walked to the station to catch our London bound train from the Margate studio, Vince told me that he had been writing a song about Imogen and Rob's last walk along the beach in Cambodia before they decided to end their lives. It was called Blue Heaven, and he said that the music was inspired by something he heard by Tears For Fears. The moment he said the words, Tears for Fears, Everybody Wants to Rule the World suddenly rang out across the train platform.

I quizzically looked for Vince's phone thinking that he was playing the Tears for Fears track out loud to illustrate his story, but no, this sound was coming from somewhere else. A group of teenagers was boarding the train and one of them was holding a vintage looking ghetto blaster, playing the 80s hit. Vince and I looked at one another and laughed incredulously. That was Imogen up to her tricks again, acknowledging her presence through the musical ether.

Spirit continues to connect us and support our individual journeys and personal growth, as does our shared love for silly and 5 rhythms dance. I treasure this embodiment of sunshine that is Vince, my soul sun, sweet spirit friend. I'm blessed to have his light in my life, and I look forward to where spirit wants to lead us next.

Cake

I remember Imogen coming home to mine extremely excited after discovering an art event after a night out in London's East End. It was called Before Encore, an art happening, exhibition event created by an artist called John Lee Bird. He painted large stylised portraits of the underground art scene, of artists, musicians, and performers of all types. At the opening of the exhibition, the subjects of the paintings would perform, creating an exciting, vibrant, cultural happening reminiscent of Warhol's Factory scene in the States.

Imogen's eyes lit up as she regaled me with stories of Le Gâteaux Chocolat (Chocolate Cake) who was a deep, velvet-voiced opera singer, chocolate skinned drag queen. There was also a Cabaret style punk band called Slapper, who's French front-man reminded Imogen of the MC from my favourite musical, Cabaret.

Slapper!

Imogen's enthusiasm for this event felt infectious, her experience there felt very reminiscent of my art school days in my youth. A few months later, John Lee Bird would attend the same gig that Imogen was playing at in a South London pub. I was there too. During Imogen's set, an intriguing camp French man, dressed in a red military style jacket and an air of the MC in Cabaret, came over to my table. He pointed at Imogen singing barefoot on stage with her red guitar, and said, "She's great, isn't she? My boyfriend, John (he gestures over to a tall, lean man with melancholic eyebrows and the air of an artist at the bar) really loves her too". "That's my baby on the stage" I stated, heart swelling with pride.

A year before my world fell apart I had a tarot reading from a friend, where she foretold of what was to come. She had interpreted what she saw in the cards as a near death of a close female, she later admitted that she had seen Imogen's death but had no idea of how to tell me in that moment. In another part of the reading, she said that in the near future I'd create my best work to date, and it would be in black and white. At the time, I thought that would be highly unlikely as I was known for my use of bold, vibrant colour. Why would I ever choose to work in black and white?

I'm a tearful mess as I stand in the corner of the dimly lit Soho club, watching models parade through the spaces between the tables, dressed in black and white clothing that bears drawings and text lifted from Imogen's notebooks. Her music plays through the speakers and a big sob erupts from my body as the final models to walk in this show appear. They are a bridal couple, both barefoot, dressed in white. Representing Imogen and Rob, they model the wedding outfits I made after their untimely deaths. Rob had asked me to make him his wedding suit before he had left for Cambodia, so I felt it was only appropriate to complete this request in his honour. The bride was wearing a dress I'd created in its entirety in one evening in an absolute frenzy. It felt like Imogen had taken over my body and using me as a tool to create her dream wedding dress. Its creation was speedy and magical. I'd used white tee shirts repurposed, and plain white muslin combined with some unique cotton lace I'd found in my local Brixton fabric shop. The lace consisted of tear drops formed into wave patterns, so poignant and perfect. These fabrics flew together, and I created a bustle from bundled muslin flanked by two appliquéd tattoo style blue birds. It was the perfect finish to the low scooped back that was the foil to the high necked front.

I had heard Imogen whisper to me from spirit to make sure her neck was covered to disguise any marks. So I obliged. Long strips of lace hung from the shoulders like extended wings and crystal tear drops adorned the breast, an echo back to my mother's own wedding dress. Lyrics from one of Imogen's songs were painted in silver along the swoop of the hip, and a tiny portrait of Rob (a facsimile of an Imogen sketch) finished the decoration. Silver Capricorn goat horns held up the simple white muslin veil, and pale blue tiny paper flowers trailed down the line of the na- ked back. It was perfect. My groom was wearing a white cotton knit tuxedo made entirely from repurposed white tees, the fitted jacket was decorated with text, line drawings and quotes from Imogen's diaries. Over the breast pocket was one of my favourite Imogen one-liners," I love cake, all kinds. " I wanted to celebrate Imogen's capacity for enjoyment in life, especially through cake, given that she went on to restrict her eating, leading to further deterioration of her mental state. The man modelling Rob's suit was my friend, Patrick.

I'd first encountered Patrick at one of John's Before Encore events. I was there with my very pregnant daughter Allegra, to support both John's amazing large- scale portraits, (of which Imogen was this time one of the subjects) and to be a proud as punch mum, watching Imogen perform some of her original songs as part of the evenings entertainment. This was at a time when Imogen was highly vulnerable, being painfully thin and very mentally unwell, but I knew that performing her music was a source of joy for her. I really appreciated John's support of my daughter's talent, he saw her light just as much as I did, but being an outsider to the family, Imogen could value his appreciation of her much more. She would always dismiss my praise with a throwaway,

"You've got to say that, you're my mother, it's your job."

This would make me smile ruefully as I realised I'd become the opposite of my mother.

My mother tried to sabotage my talent, thank goodness I'd broken that cycle.

Allegra and I were waiting for Imogen's performance to begin, and we sat on a sofa next to a big bowl of peanuts. A very handsome older man, a cross between David Bowie and Clint Eastwood, started sharing the peanuts and some high-energy banter with us, regaling us with stories with his youthful and slightly crazy energy. We both took to him immediately, and he became a friend from that moment on. He felt familiar to us, one of us, gooble gabble.

Patrick was Swedish and, during his heyday in the 70s and 80s, a successful International model, travelling the world and rubbing shoulders with the party scene of New York's most beautiful people. Patrick had stories and scandals in abundance and a youthful exuberance that belied his years. He was a decade older than me, but I felt very much like I was his big sister. We would go on to play dress up with my wearable art, and I'd snap his effortless poses on my iPhone. It was clear that Patrick still had much to contribute to the world of modelling. We'd meet regularly for a ritual of dry cappuccino and carrot cake at our local Italian coffee shop, cake once again becoming an important way of celebrating life. It's the simple things that create glimmers of joy, so needed in these increasingly tough times. I'm sure Imogen and Patrick's beloved mumma are up there somewhere, mapping out our next adventures over some good cake.

58

Finding My Voice

It would be Patrick's teasing ways and unfiltered manner that would help me unpack an aspect of my autistic self that I hadn't given too much thought to.

It was during one of our many telephone calls that he would point out to me every few minutes that my way of speaking would change. Apparently, he could hear me go from received English BBC tones, then shift over to a more South London accent.

Every few sentences, he'd point out the shift as I tried to speak about something very intense I was currently focusing on. I could feel my anger building as he found my voice changing more and more amusing.

I was not laughing.

In fact, I had got myself into a proper state and soon hot, furious tears of frustration were pouring down my cheeks as I tried to express just how frustrated I was becoming.

But of course, my voice, in its emotional state, kept shifting tone and Patrick was hyper-fixated on pointing it out to me. Eventually, I managed to get his attention and he realised I was genuinely upset.

As difficult as this moment was for me, it highlighted the fact that if I became too aware of the sound of my voice, I found it almost impossible to speak. I had the same issue when it came to breathing in any meditation practice. As soon as I was given the instruction to focus on my breath, I would panic and not know how to breathe.

Patrick had uncovered my very obvious echolalia. Echolalia is the unsolicited repetition of vocalisations made by another person, often connected with autism. Mine seemed to be attached to accents. When working as a children's entertainer, I'd typically find myself unconsciously imitating my French client's accent when in conversation. It is very hard not to appear to be mocking, so this was rather embarrassing. Of course, in the context of my voicing multiple puppet characters, this shifting voice cadence came to be very useful indeed.

I've never had a clear accent that anyone can pin down. I can trace this back to my mother not letting me play with the local Midlands kids lest I get to sound like them. Mum associated regional accents with being lower class, and she was determined to escape her working-class roots. So I went from an indeterminate Midlands voice to Cape Town, South Africa. The combination of these two accents being closer to received English than I probably realised.

If identity has to do with accent, I'm a confused woman. I think this is why I feel I cannot speak if I'm forced to focus on how I sound. I lose all sense of self, including my voice.

Mimicking animal sounds makes me happier, more than it should. I'm happiest when on a farm among a flock of sheep or goats, failing that a rafter of turkeys, where I can gobble to my heart's content. For me, I thoroughly enjoy the call and response game that is triggered once you manage to correctly mimic each individual animal's voice. I realise that not many people will appreciate this very quirky side of me, but it brings me deep joy.

Dr Doolittle must have been autistic!
Gooble gobble, Mr Turkey, we accept him, one of us, one of us.

59

I Am An Artist

It's 2013, I had just received the news of my dear daddy's death from emphysema.

A life-long heavy smoker, dad's lungs would inevitably bear the brunt and end up being his way out of life. My inner child sighed.

If only Daddy had paid attention to the warnings she had scribbled on his cigarette packets.

This would be my very first experience of looking death in the face.

I walked the long, gloomy pale green corridor in the bowels of the hospital, following the signs that said Mortuary. My heart was in my mouth and my brain was in complete denial as I put one foot in front of the other on this seemingly endless journey to say my last goodbye. Surely, this was a mistake, a dream perhaps? Maybe I would wake up in a few more steps?

The nurse who met me popped me out of my bubble of denial as she led me into the room where they had prepared Dad's body for viewing. She said she'd wait for me outside, and she apologised for the fact that Dad wasn't able to close his mouth, it being a normal consequence of the death process.

Dad knew his time was nigh, he had called me a week before he died and had insisted about talking over his funeral plans, despite my feeble attempt to change the subject.

"Keep it simple, Di," he'd said.

Dad had always been a humble man, kind, with simple tastes and a deep love of fishing. After our conversation, he had managed to distract the rest of the immediate family in the Midlands by agreeing to be moved into sheltered accommodation where his oxygen needs could be monitored more closely. My aunt, uncle, and cousins were busy sorting out new carpets and curtains for his new room. While they were busy, Dad quietly died at home in his sleep. He got what he wanted ultimately, no fuss. He was a 'not bothered' kind of guy.

So here he lies, mouth open as the nurse had warned me.

Goodnight, I love you, God bless.

Words chanted
A nighttime mantra
Rhythm of words that needed to be said
Accompanied by sloppy kisses that made me screw up my face It always made you chuckle, as you tucked me into bed. Goodnight, sweet, silly Daddy,
This final parting is tough
You were always there for me
When life's seas were rough
It was you who would calm me if I saw monsters at night
It was you I came running to if I got a fright.
I love you gentle daddy, you taught me lessons about the earth
About beauty in nature, its value and its worth.
Your stillness sat on the river bank waiting for the float to bob
I have so much to thank you for
Your light heartedness and humour,
Your silly sausage ways
Your handsprings on the beach in your younger days.
We climbed the trees together, took hammers to the rocks
To crack open, finding wonderment or sometimes nasty shocks
Of a spider or an insect that you'd tease me with
God bless you, silly daddy, if I only could believe.
We didn't go for God stuff much
Makes it harder now to grieve.

But I'll see you in the rustling trees
And hear you in the wind
And smell you in the damp woodland
And feel you in the breeze.
Good night sweet, silly Daddy.
I love you
God Bless.

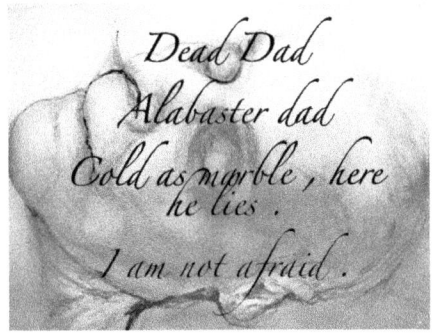

Dead Dad
Alabaster dad
Cold as marble, here he lies.
I am not afraid.

As I sat with my dad's ice-cold, still body, I searched for him. It became increasingly obvious that he wasn't there. This cold spaceship was his container. His spirit had clearly left. The thing that made him him was no longer.

As I continued to search for him by tracing my finger along the familiar outline of his nose, I said out loud,

" This is your nose, but it's not your nose."

Then his ear that bore lobes just like mine:

"This is your ear, but it's not your ear."

I became overwhelmingly, exquisitely aware of the absence of his presence.

It was at that point in my quest to find him that I heard it:

Dad's voice.

" Do it now, Di! Don't die with regret. We get one shot at life, so whatever you're holding back on, do it now! "

I became acutely aware, as his only child, that I would most probably be next on that marble slab. (God willing)

Facing my mortality in such a physical way seemed to snap me out of a deep slumber, as if some ghostly hypnotist had just snapped their fingers, releasing me from the trance.

I knew right away that when I got home, I was going to jump off that cliff and free-fall into being an artist.

No more excuses, no more, "This is still creative,"

I was going to abandon the kids' entertainment job at the pinnacle of my success and throw myself into my true joyful destiny of being and living as an artist. At the ripe old age of 49, I'd finally got there with my dad's help, at least in intention.

One of the first things I did when I got back home was take selfies in front of the various pieces of my art on my walls at home, each time announcing out loud to the ether: I am an artist!

I posted this collection of photos to my social media for accountability, in an album titled, "I am an artist."

All of my friends and followers casually commented, yes of course you are, we've always known that.

Isn't always the way, that we are the last to know?

Not long after this public declaration I would meet my art mentor and friend, my Queen of Cups, Sue Kreitzman.

Within a year, I'd find myself hand in hand with Sue, marching down the graffiti'd Leake Street tunnels in London's Waterloo dressed in all our splendour, followed behind by a gaggle of creatives.

We chanted in unison,

"One of us, One of us, We accept her, We accept her, one of us, Gooble Gabble,"

as the beat of the drummer, echoing in the tunnel, became the heartbeat of our intention.

I'd done it, here I am!

I am an artist!

60

Little Dead Wren and the Rollercoaster

It was a regular sunny afternoon in 2013 and time to take my dog for a walk again.

Everything in my life was strangely calm at this point.

After the death of my dad, things seemed to be falling in to place. Even Imogen seemed happy, her new boy-friend, Rob, had taken her off to Thorpe park so they could indulge in the rollercoasters for the day.

As I walked past the window in the communal stairwell of my block of flats, my eye caught something unusual. At first glance, I thought it was a large dead bumblebee, they'd often fly in and end their lives on the window ledge, but this was a little too big for a bee. On closer inspection, the 'bee' turned out to be a tiny, perfectly formed dead bird. I couldn't just leave it there, so I brought it back in to my flat, placed it carefully into a matchbox and left to walk the dog once more. When I returned, I drew and painted this little creature from many angles, in some sort of attempt to honour its life. It was such an unusual discovery, I can't say I'd ever seen such a tiny perfect bird before.

Finding it somehow felt significant. What was the message that this tiny bird was trying to deliver?

I did a bit of research and found out that this was a wren, fully grown, probably it had flown into the window pane and knocked itself unconscious, consequently dying.

As always, I looked into the spiritual meaning of this bird.

The message I received was that because of this bird's rollercoaster shaped flight path and melodic song, it was considered to be a connector of creatives, especially poets, songwriters, artists, musicians, and authors.

After I had painted this tiny bird, I packed it up carefully in a matchbox and cottonwool, and posted it off to a taxidermist who made beautiful art from ethically sourced deceased animals. After all this ceremony, I simply couldn't just discard this tiny creature.

A few days later, I took my then 3-year-old granddaughter, Erykah, on a treasure hunt around the local charity shop. I told her she could choose something for herself. After a little while, she came to the till with a small framed picture clutched tightly against her chest. She said she'd found her 'special bird' and she'd fallen in love with this little painting. When I could prise it away from her chest, the bird painting revealed itself to be a wren, in fact, the word 'wren' was written in pencil on the back.

In the evening of the day I found my wren, I had called Imogen to find out about her day at the Theme Park.

She excitedly regaled me with a story about a tiny bird that had flown in front of her face in a rollercoaster type flight path. She said she'd looked it up and found out it was a wren.

Synchronicity and signposts everywhere.

Three years later after Imogen's death, creatives of all types would reach out to me to send condolences and express just how much Imogen had meant to them.

She had no idea just how wide her influence had spread, especially in the Indie music scene. It seemed that she had connected creatives in a wren-like fashion, herself.

My connecting creatives went into full force in 2016 after the StyleLikeU interview.

I was one among many interesting humans who had sat on a stool and told their story whilst taking off layers of clothing.

Another was Tarriona ' Tank' Ball, the driving force behind the Grammy award-winning New Orleans band, Tank and the Bangas.

After watching her interview, I immediately warmed to this deeply soulful and authentic human. I went away to look up her music out of curiosity and a new love affair with their music, but especially the poetry found in her lyrics, began. Her words would give me goosebumps and bring me to tears.

Last night, just before performing my favourite of their songs, Rollercoasters, Tank took to the mic, calling me up to the stage. I presented her with an exceptional robe created to mark the pinnacle of every musicians' achievement, the winning of a coveted Grammy Award. It felt both magical and inevitable because from the very start of my discovering her talent, I knew she was destined to be at this very place. Deep in my bones I knew that one day her star would shine bright.

The brown and gold sequinned kimono dazzled under the stage lights as Tank stretched out her arms displaying the long sleeved, highly decorated robe, and the crowd cheered. She turned around to reveal a hand-painted portrait of herself in her sequinned dress, on the night she became a Grammy winner in the category of Spoken Word.

This robe was the latest in a growing collection that I'd made Tank and her band-mates over the past six years. Tank would start up a tradition of gifting personalised robes that I'd make to her nearest and dearest, including Jill Scott, (another Grammy winner) Lalah Hathaway and Norah Jones.

Poets and artists, musicians and creatives of all types are now linked together across the globe through these robes, all of them containing my creative energy and positive intention.

That little dead bird knew what it was doing, the evidence of its connective power was right here. A tiny feathered prayer, come to deliver a message of hope and possibility. Thank you, little wren, thank you, Tank and thank you to my higher self for being open enough to respond to the wren's call to action.

61

The Final Artwork

Trigger warning. This chapter deals with detailed discussion of a double suicide

Tegan didn't know Imogen, but somehow Imogen used Tegan to send messages to me through dreams.

27th November 2019.
Messenger message:

Tegan: Okay, so again I was dreaming of speaking with Imogen and I sort of don't want to tell you this because it's difficult, but I will. I'm going to need a day or two to steady myself, if that's okay. I love her, but she's HARD work, Diane, and I have no idea why it's me she's talking to in my dreams. You know this already, I know it. Actually screw that. I know exactly why she's talking to me. I've just realised, in part at least.

Me: Oh my! She is hard work, but that work is important. I am keen to hear. She recently 'haunted' another friend of mine for a while, she would sit in the corner of the room, head down face covered with her thick hair, drawing in the carpet with her finger. She was actually

looking after this friend as she was also going through similar struggles to Imogen, being undiagnosed autistic.
(This friend has since been diagnosed autistic.)

Tegan: Okay, I have a weird question. In my dream, she had a sort of way of holding herself, like she'd almost tilt her head to one side as she talks. It was really peculiar and the sort of gesture that would make sense if I could describe it. I can't really, like she was thinking hard about everything she said that was significant.

Me: It's going to sound gruesome, but she did hang herself and her head was in that position. Everything is significant, she's managed to get through, so she needs to make sure everything is right.

Tegan: No it's fine, and it's sort of about that actually… that she wanted to talk to me about and, I was like, nope, nope I'm not talking to your mum about that. Not about this, babe. I'm so sorry.

Me: Was she worried about the photo?

Imogen and Rob hanged themselves together in a peculiar, ritualised way out in Cambodia. They were found blindfolded, gagged, had their holding hands bound together, and the other hand bound behind their backs. Their legs were taped together. Because of the obvious involvement of a third party (it is physically impossible to achieve this without help) their deaths were initially suspected as murder. After a lengthy and thorough investigation, involving Imogen's notebooks, lyric book and suicide notes) it became quite evident that this was a carefully crafted, meticulously staged, assisted double suicide.
I had sent Imogen money a week before she did this on her 28th birthday.
In Cambodia, it is very possible to use money to get assistance to do something like this. I've even read in some tourist guidebooks to Cambodia, words to the effect that the police there are as corrupt as you can afford. Part

of this corrupt environment was the fact that suicides and other death scenes were photographed and sold on to various International news outlets. It was because of this that a photo of Imogen and Rob's death was depicted on the Internet.

I've written, begged, pleaded with and cajoled various blogs and Google headquarters itself to try to get this photo taken down. It sadly remains as a gruesome and tasteless memorial to what was meant to be a secret and private departure, far away from the eyes of those they could hurt.

Found in Imogen's diary when she was 16

Tegan: Yes, yes she was worried about the photograph!

Me: I thought she might be

Tegan: Oh but there's so much more.

Me: She never intended us to see, you know?

Tegan: No, she absolutely didn't at all, and I don't think she realised the upset it would cause, but also she was telling me that she HAD to, and that she never felt such, (and honestly, I don't even want to use this word) but comfort? It was this that she was talking about last time too, Diane, but I didn't want to say too much.

Me: Was she saying it brought her peace?

Tegan: Yes, but I was a little bit spun out, I still am. I told her, look I'm glad you're okay, but I can't help. I'm not the right person to talk to here.

Me: I've been following the teachings of the Law of Attraction(Abraham Hicks). In it, they teach that we make too much of the death process, they say that at the moment of death we become immediately aligned with our higher selves and Source, which is like the ultimate coming home feeling: a feeling of pure bliss and expansiveness. I've experienced a bit of this myself through meditation and dance, most people have to die to experience this bliss, so I know what she is talking about.

Tegan: That makes sense.

Me: It's also the reason I can talk to people about Imogen's death with joy as I know she is good. This is why she keeps sending us these messages, she's desperate to let us know she is okay.

Tegan: She made me promise to tell you that she's okay, basically. She did the most utterly bizarre thing. I have a comfort blanket that I've had since infancy, it's one of the few things that brings me physical comfort if I need it. She made me promise in this dream. I said," I don't understand, Imogen, I'm scared, I'm not with you, I don't know what you mean!" She said, "Trust me, when you wake, you'll understand what this comfort means." I said, "I don't believe you, but okay." She said, "Promise me, trust me on it," and I turned away. As I woke up, I suddenly under- stood what she meant by comfort, as she made me aware of my blanket. It's all so gory and in depth and grisly, but she is desperately trying to get me to talk to you about this.

Me : She was into some dark stuff and self harmed, so it doesn't really surprise me, to be honest.

Tegan: I was trying to explain to her how this may be upsetting for you to hear, and she was getting frustrated with me for not listening.

Me: Imogen's key emotion was frustration. She struggled a lot with miscommunication and not being understood.

Tegan: So I just had to trust her, the girl doesn't shy away from gore, I get that now. I'm guessing that was just part of her, well... 'herness', but I'd deliver the message as I wouldn't want to piss her off.

Me: Thank you for being willing to pass on the message, and I'm sorry she's such a bugger. But that's my Imogen! She was difficult, brilliant, beautiful, perfect, irritating, all of the above, a dark genius. I'm not all that bothered about the details, I already knew them. I've seen the photo. The reason she's pulled you in to being involved is because you were there when that magic happened. You saw the magic, so she must've seen you. She was clearly in the room that evening when Scout was there because the butterfly came earlier, so...

Do you know, when I heard the details of how they were found, the bondage and blindfolds, I knew that was all Imogen. I knew that was her because she liked to research and plan right down to the last detail. Everything was deliberate and considered so that things would go right. And they did.

Tegan: Yes, that's basically it... It all went perfectly right, and she hoped you saw that and knew that and...yeah.

Me: If I know my Imogen, she wants me to be proud of her for her final artwork.

Tegan: YES, YES! She absolutely does! And she is proud of it, too.

Me: I am, though. I know it sounds morbid, but I am proud of her. It was the darkest poetry.

Tegan, No, no, I understand it.

DISCLAIMER:

These thoughts were written post Imogen's death when there was no way of undoing or preventing what she did. This was my way of unpacking the complex emotions that are left behind after a loss by suicide.

I am not promoting nor condoning the taking of life by one's own hand or otherwise. Life is precious and needs to be cherished. If you, dear reader, have any dark thoughts of your own, hold on, distract yourself anyway you can. Tell someone you trust. Remember, you are the blue sky. The despair is the weather, the storm clouds that will pass by if you can only but shelter and wait it out.

You are important, you are valued just for the fact that you exist. You matter. You are loved. Let's try to squeeze as much bliss out of our time here on earth be- fore we head home. Let's enjoy this wonderful, magical mystery tour together.

62

A Conversation with a former Skeptic

On Butterflies and Countdown miracles

John, a mutual friend of Imogen and Rob, messaged me about a year after their deaths.

He spoke of how he was struggling to understand or make sense of their decisions to end things. He wanted to try to gain some sense of closure.

I deeply empathised with this stranger, as of course, there had been no funeral in the UK to help friends of Imogen and Rob process their passing. John and I began to discuss his logical way of looking at the world, and how this way of thinking had been gently challenged by his seeing signs and messages since their deaths.

J: Did I tell you about our phone?

Me: No?

J: She lent me an old android phone. She'd wiped her personal data but the auto-correct's memory would give me oblique insights into her life. Sometimes it felt like divining or holding a possessed object. It was special to me.

Me: Oh! That is SO Imogen. That pleases me greatly.

J: I'm a rationalist but willing to be proven wrong on a lot of my beliefs but even from a rational perspective, there was something to it. We lived through our words, and there was a remnant of the way she used words.

Taking a break here to give the reader a sample of how Imogen used words:

Four-Letter Word

So tonight, before I folded myself into bed
There were words I wanted to give you
*   My tongue rolled them around my mouth*
I held three in each cheek
Like confessions, they danced nervous to my teeth
Then back into my throat
I swallowed them whole
Because it's already so obvious what I meant,
With every hug and all the straining of my cheek muscles.

As a word, it's too restricting
So when I finally let it slip don't think that I didn't wish I did
I'd write it on your wrist before you did
And when you awoke we'd both know
You mean more to me than a word could ever be.

And back to the conversation.

Me: She's around us still. I hear you on the rationalist thing, but Imogen's death has blown my logical world apart because we've had so many signs from her that I've had to suspend disbelief. I now believe in a higher power, I call it Source. She's come to me and her sister in dreams on the same night, reassuring us both that she is okay. I've had a peacock butterfly that keeps coming to visit me. I had one that seemed to manifest out of thin air in my bathroom in November, before I was about to go to a Scout Niblett concert.

Imogen always said I needed to go and see Scout live if I could. Somehow, by what seemed like divine intervention, through a friend called Tegan, I ended up on Scout's guest list.

There was a particular song that Imogen had recorded out in Cambodia that I had on the flash drive, called It's Time. We all loved it so much and we knew all the lyrics. It seemed to poetically describe Imogen and Rob's journey through addiction out there in Cambodia. The producer of the documentary we were making about Imogen asked me to copyright all of Imogen's songs so that they could be used for the soundtrack. It's Time was an obvious choice for the film. I tried over and over to get this done, but the Universe kept blocking me at every turn. By the time I went to the gig, I still hadn't managed to complete it.

At the gig, Scout sang It's Time.

*I*t turns out that Imogen had covered Scout's song, after seeing a live YouTube performance of this new song when she was out in Cambodia. No wonder the Universe wasn't allowing me to copyright it. Imogen wouldn't let me.

Earlier, while getting ready for the gig, the peacock butterfly had landed on my naked belly and opened up its wings as it rested on my womb space, such a magical, mysterious moment.

J: Scout Niblett is good, and I knew she was important to Imo.

Me: Strange occurrences were myriad. Immediately after her death, when her energy was clearly chaotic and desperate, my television would switch on and off by itself. My lights would flicker, a drinking glass exploded right in front of me as it sat on a side table. Robins would drop like stones out of the trees and sit next to my feet in the park. Blue tits would follow me as I walked in the park. Allegra had a large moth that wouldn't leave her front door, despite her shooing it away. A month before Imogen died, I heard a voice in my flat saying SURRENDER. It bounced off the wall of my living room, growing louder and louder until I was forced to respond to it.

"Okay, I fucking surrender! Let what will come, let it come!"

As soon as those words spilled across my lips, I realised what I had done. I had just let Imogen go. I think I had just agreed to complete my part of what I now believe is my soul contract with Imogen. Hidden in an anagram in her name is the message:
I'm gone, A kiss, A God lie.
From that moment on I became a spiritual being because there is no denying that she is still here.

To conclude our chat, I offered John an Angel oracle card reading. He was very open to receiving this. It led him to say to me that he was prepared to drop the cynicism and step into an open-heart space. I told him that this was a wonderful decision, as belief was the frequency of spiritual connection.

Later on that afternoon, I wrote this:

Me: As I'm walking down the street to pick up my grandson from nursery, I'm filled with an overwhelming sensation of "THANK YOU MUM!" It's almost unbearable. The love they're sending right now for you through me is intense. It's both of them. This is why I'm finding it difficult to hold. It's dissipating now... phew, that was intense. I was walking down the road and it just sort of welled up inside of me after a wave of full-body goosebumps. It was an intense sensation of love. I've had goosebumps before, but this was different, as if it was both of them eager to con- nect with you. So both moving through my body at the same time. I think that they saw it was starting to overwhelm me, I mean, imagine having the equivalent of having a massive orgasm in the middle of the street, a bit awkward! But then as I gathered my senses, it started to rain, which literally put a dampener on things. If I were to summarise your reading, it would be this:

To get to the ultimate wisdom, you need to have the courage to completely surrender reason to achieve a state of awakening, finding the truth of your soul.

J: I feel a change on my side and this has helped me find some peace. Suffice it to say they are welcome to try to contact me personally.

Me: When you go to bed, set the intention to chat with them in your dreams. Trust me, they're so happy you've reached out.

The next day
J: Strange night, good night! It would be interesting to talk to you about it.

Me: Have you felt a shift around their transition into the non-physical? How do your insides feel now about them not being here in the flesh? Has there been any change since we last spoke? I have just had clear communication from the both of them that they are eager for you to know that they are well and that it is possible to feel them if you are open to it.
Put yourself in Rob's shoes, how are you able as a spiritual energy to help your friend know that you see him?

J: Diane!! I literally wear his shoes every day!

Me: Oh, that's beautiful! Words, words are the route in here... they were both such wordsmiths.

J: I'm trying to find a way to show you what I saw on a rerun of Countdown this morning.

John then managed to send me a recording of that morning's Countdown Conundrum.

It went a little like this:
Presenter: Now we go in for our tea time teaser which is ICE DIE WED.

The clue is: It sounds like both of us made the joint decision to put lots of chemicals up the garden path.

(Advert break)

Welcome back! It sounds like both of us made the joint decision to put lots of chemicals up the garden path.
And the answer to that one is (sharp intake of breath) WEEDICIDE

Then it sounds like he says WE DECIDE (and chuckles)

The message from them through word play on their favourite geeky TV program couldn't have been more clear and pertinent.

John had asked me to give him clarity over why they had decided to do what they did, and there was an unspoken query around if it had anything to do with their friends. Guilt and bargaining after suicide are very common emotions. This not so cryptic message explained that it was solely Imogen and Rob's responsibility that they had decided for their reasons, and their reasons only.

They used drugs secretly ICE (' leading' up the garden path)
They died, DIE, after they got married, WED.
The phrase : putting lots of chemicals up the garden path? Well, none of us knew about their secret heroin addiction. Then the reveal, why did they do it? They made a joint decision ...

WE DECIDE.

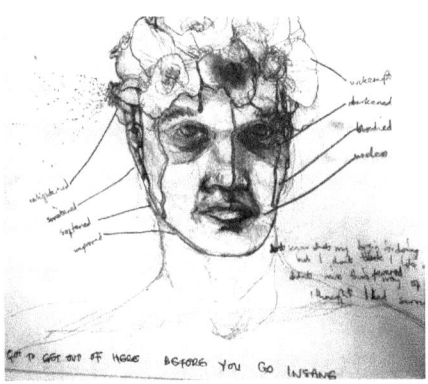

And if you don't believe me, feel free to look it up.
Countdown on demand, 8th October 2019

63

On Being a Grandma

One of the biggest secrets hidden from all mothers is the absolute joy that can be found upon becoming a grandparent.

GRANDMA, what a loaded word.

Ageism and misogyny informs us in its propagandising manner that this title is to be feared and avoided, instead substituting titles like Nana or heaven forbid, 'Glamma', lest you accept the curse of being perceived as old. I challenge any mother facing this fear to let go and embrace the beautiful gift that is to be a grandparent.

What an honour it is to be in the position to show your grandchildren all the fun and exciting things in life that exist on the peripherals of everyday parenting. Here is an opportunity to introduce magic into your family's lives, to move through the world that inspires young minds. This is an invitation to show the new generation the treasures discovered along your life's journey and an opportunity for you to see life through their brand new fresh eyes.

I became a grandma at a young age. At the time my Allegra told me she was pregnant, I was preparing to tell her that I was possibly pregnant too. (It turns out it was perimenopause). My beautiful daughter, soon to be become a mother, was just 17 when she told me. I was thrown into shock and panic at first and had to come face to face with my own internalised misogyny as I jumped immediately into judgement and shame. I felt as if I had failed as a mother. After many tears and conversations, I was able to regroup and start to change my knee-jerk attitude and gear up for what was to become a very dramatic journey into grand-parenthood.

During Allegra's time of pregnancy, Imogen was going through an intense period of struggle with her mental health. She was, at that time, living with her boyfriend and his family after dropping out of University, following three months of struggle, failing to adjust to the boozy and chaotic student scene that was campus life. After being at Uni for a few months, she announced to me that she had got a job in a bookshop and was leaving University. My initial response was disappointment at the loss of such an opportunity. Imogen had been on the prestigious creative writing course at University of East Anglia, and we had such dreams for her. Imogen was the first in the family to go to University, so she must have felt enormous pressure. I quickly realised just how much her mental health had declined since starting out there a mere three months earlier. She had done the right thing for her. No-one should have to go through such struggle.

After her death, I would come across a song she wrote during this time, the lyrics explain exactly how she was feeling and why she came to the decision to leave.

Get Out

I need to tell you what I really mean
That kind of life has never been me
I spent so long trying to work out if I should stay or leave
But pretty soon I knew that kind of life, it just isn't me.
So when you go, figure out how it will feel
To be six thousand pounds in debt for just three years of drinking cheap vodka

And pretending to like people you'd never even want to meet.
You know, they've lied, you don't need this,
You could put all this time into something or someone, or somewhere you love,
 And eventually, you will find a satisfying job.
Or at least if you don't you're happy and free in the comfort of saying who you
 want to be
I'm not trying to say that no-one gets a kick out of pretending to be confident
 and secretly resenting those people who get you into drinking and vacuous laughing and the desperate pursuit of friends.
 Love who you love and don't pretend.
And what of the love you leave behind?
Leaving just to favour a life of slavery to debt repayments
And pushing for promotions to get some appreciation for whom you work for.
But ultimately, none of that life is yours.
Your money, your house, your family, your spouse,
owned entirely by a string of interest and obligations and consumption.
I don't know why you're all so excited to leave.
My advice to you would be to get out while you still can.
Get out, get out, get out, get out.

The Imogen that returned from a brief stint at University was markedly different. She was painfully thin with angry self harm marks on her arms. She had started seeing a psychiatrist to support her mental health struggles, and she had been started on Prozac, but it really didn't appear to be helping her at all. In fact, it seemed to make her far worse.

Imogen then started turning up randomly at my home, bingeing, purging then leaving. I think she was trying to show me her struggles. I felt totally helpless.

My attention was torn between my younger pregnant daughter who was about to sit her A-levels, and my older, mentally unwell daughter who was spiralling down into a very dark place. At that point, I was relying on the expertise of the doctors and psychiatrists and I encouraged Imogen to keep on taking her medication. I also offered for Imogen to come and live back home with me, but she turned it down.

It turned out that she was really struggling in her relationship and she eventually asked me to help her leave, which I did. I became the bad guy, the one to blame for the break-up, so that Imogen had a clear exit strategy.

Things became extremely intense and stayed that way. I worried I'd lose my eldest just as my youngest was about to give birth, somehow she managed to get herself through.

By this stage, she'd been medicated with anti-psychotics and mood stabilisers that made her violently shake. It terrified her, but in my ignorance I asked her to keep on taking the pills. After all, didn't the doctor's know best?

Studies have now shown that autistic people can react very differently to medication. Our nervous systems are different, so that makes sense. (Gaeun Park et al, Dysregulation of the signalling pathway (Experimental & Molecular Medicine 2023)

Imogen at that time had been diagnosed with ' Rapid Cycling Bipolar Disorder ' and Borderline Personality Disorder. It turns out that this is a very common misdiagnosis pathway for many highly masked autistic women before they finally are diagnosed properly with autism. It makes me sad to know that so many women and girls have gone through the same torturous journey that Imogen went through.

By the time Imogen took her life in 2016, attitudes towards neurodivergent women had started to shift, sadly far too late for Imogen. There are still cases of young autistic women locked up in psychiatric units across the UK today just for having issues with eating. ARFID (Avoidant Restrictive Food Intake Disorder) often linked to autism, can often be mistaken for anorexia. It is entirely different with different drivers. ARFID is anxiety and sensory based, typically around new textures of food and inconsistency of fresh food, requiring a gentle and compassionate approach, certainly not force-feeding.

I'm grateful for the fact that as we are learning more about neurodivergence, we have language to criticise the system and greater support our neurodivergent women and girls who were previously rendered invisible.

There is so much still to be done.

Allegra gave birth to Erykah-Rose, and I was so privileged to be there. I'm glad I was because Erykah almost died. She was born rapidly after a painful induced labour and the midwife (who spent most of her time on Facebook) wrapped up the baby, setting her under the warming lamp and left. I was left alone with this new precious bundle and my exhausted, sleeping daughter. I quickly realised something was wrong as Erykah was making strange grunting noises and was starting to go blue. Running out into the corridor in a panic, I shouted for help. Little Erykah was rushed up to the Special Care Baby Unit and placed immediately on a ventilator.

Whispers around the unit in the following few days would reveal that "That was the baby that almost died." During her stay in the unit, it was picked up that our sweet baby also had a bowel condition that needed corrective surgery when she was three months old.

Once baby was well enough to go home, Allegra and I became experts at administering baby enemas to keep her comfortable before she had surgery. The surgery went well and now Erykah-Rose is a completely healthy child. It turns out it was a good thing we spent some time in the Special Care Baby Unit after all, as things may have gone differently if we had just taken her home.

Quickly it became evident that Erykah was special. I remember Allegra's behaviour being challenging as she grew out of her placid babyhood, but Erykah took things to new levels. She would go on to teach us about compassion, patience, resilience and our own neurodivergence. She would also teach us about changing perspective.

Just like the hanging man in the Tarot, hanging upside down from one leg, observing life from a new angle, she ultimately taught us how to surrender to seeing things in a new way. Her stuckness and inability to adapt to our expectations, forced us to soften into a new way of being.

Just like a caterpillar dissolving into chemical soup inside the chrysalis to reconfigure into a butterfly, this transformation would be chaotic, painful and force us to surrender. When Erykah was five, she was introduced to her new baby brother Oliver, who would go on to become both her friend and unintentional trigger as Ollie's neurodivergence presented as high energy and lots of vocal stimming.

The Universe had created a family with two children on the opposing sides of the sensory needs spectrum.

This would turn out to be highly challenging, but it is really lovely to see my grandchildren grow up to really like and respect one another's differences, well, mostly. As a family, we could ensure that our youngest members had the full knowledge and support of their neurodivergence, both of them receiving diagnoses early on. This provided them a framework to be able to understand themselves as perfectly neurodivergent rather than feeling like broken neurotypicals.

I know that some people disapprove of labels. I've heard them described beautifully as being just like care labels in our laundry. Happiness and self-love can only come from viewing yourself through a clear lens in my experience. I have really appreciated observing the different unmasked behaviours in my grandchildren. This has allowed me to identify similar ones in myself, which in turn allows me to make peace with the associated behaviours and accommodate for my needs now I really understand them in a new and healthy way.

Self Portrait at 60 (on being self diagnosed autistic)

I mogen was our canary in the coal mine, she started us on the path to our awareness of neurodivergence.

Erykah and Ollie have since helped light the way.

Interpersonal family relationships within our tiny family have completely shifted for the better, as we can now understand previously criticised behaviours with a lot more compassion and clarity as to the root cause. This simple mind shift has changed everything.

I've self diagnosed as Autistic and ADHD (AUDHD) as I can clearly see the elements of both Imogen, Ollie and Erykah in myself. I don't feel compelled to get a formal diagnosis at this late stage of my life, as my lifestyle as an artist means I do not need extra workplace support or accommodations.

My mental health has improved immensely since I've been aware of honouring my sensory needs, giving myself adequate downtime to recover from overstimulating social situations. I've also given myself permission to stop people pleasing, focusing in on my needs. This simple shift has had the greatest impact of all. Living for myself, outwards, has meant I've been able to create healthy boundaries, and I've found the ability to say no. Obviously, life still has its challenges, it always will, it's part of the agreement we made before choosing to come into this dimension. At least now, I don't take things so personally any more. Rather than bending towards everyone else, I've learned to be a rock and allow the chaos of life to swirl around me. If it still goes wrong, I've always got the dance and a nice cup of tea.

64

Home

As a young woman, I would hear people talking about taking time out to 'find themselves' and I would inwardly scoff. The whole concept seemed ridiculous to me, what self was there to find? Are we not always with ourselves? As a child, there were hints that things might not be that simplistic, as I'd hear my mother's frustrated cry to the empty room,

" Where's Sandra gone? "

Hearing this as a small child confused me.
My inner voice would silently answer her, "You're right there, Mummy."
Of course, looking back at my mother's plaintive query, it's quite evident to my adult self that my mother was having a crisis of identity, having found herself thrust into the drudgery of motherhood. The change must've been difficult for her to embrace, as I knew mum really understood herself primarily through the male gaze.

She would go on to have similar struggles as she went through menopause, where the hormonal changes took her right back to her self-loathing fat child self. Mum couldn't accept her body being anything but skinny because skinny meant fuckable and fuckable meant she existed.

I've always lived in a larger body, as I've never dared restrict food. If I do, I end up becoming very rigid, and it's easy for me to slip over into ARFID (avoidant restrictive food intake disorder) territory, just like Imogen did.

Mum really hated seeing my comfort in my own skin as a larger bodied woman. She would constantly comment on my weight and throw nasty comments at me when she felt fit. I think I triggered her own self loathing that she projected straight on to me. My response to continuous nasty commentary about my body when she was staying with me during that fateful last visit, was to make sure I deliberately walked around naked in my own home. That way, defying her critical gaze and challenging her through exposure.

It seemed to work to a larger extent, as she finally admitted that my body was quite nice as it was in proportion. That was the closest to a compliment I'd ever got from her on my physical appearance.

I think I had become a walking, talking, living, breathing trigger for her. I chalked this up as a small win as I realised I'd started to accept my body as it was, as my home.
Was this part of finding myself? I wasn't sure, but I suspected it may have been.

I was to discover my hidden self that I had carefully hidden away for most of my life, so well that I had no concept of ever being missing, once grief blew apart my very stable 13 year relationship.

I'd never lived alone until that point, I'd gone from my family home, to flat share, to being a serial monogamist, always having a live-in partner, continually over a period of 31 years. Once I was forced into a place of solitude, (I needed to be alone to process such deep grief that is losing a child to suicide) I started to unmask. Not that I knew that this was what I was doing, mind you. It was purely situational, not having to think about another's needs, meant for the very first time in my life, I focused on my own. Things started to fall into place as I realised that when I was cohabiting, I would be acting out the role of the wife/ partner, and would automatically drop into stereotypical behaviours of a mother hen role.

My last healthy partner was puzzled by this. Although he benefited from my domestic fussing persona I'd adopted, he instinctively knew that that wasn't my authentic self and would constantly tell me that I really didn't need to do it. But I couldn't not. With the hindsight of the understanding of my autism, I can see that I was just following the social rules, learned from watching my mother. Not once in all this time did I realise that I had an option not to do things that way.

Not having a partner in my living space gave me the permission to start again, already being in deep grief meant that I didn't have the capacity to mourn the loss of that relationship at the time. The inability to hyper focus on losing my relationship meant I was able to focus on my day-to-day life, and choose a way of living that brought gentleness and comfort to my soul.

I let go of any expectations of how I was supposed to be and allowed myself to just exist in the moment.
Grief really helped me unmask.

I look back now and understand with absolute clarity my fight/ flight response to the sound of gunshots and car chases in the movies he used to watch. Now I understood why I'd react so badly to his sudden excited outbursts when he watched his favourite football team play. I wasn't being grumpy, unreasonable or a killjoy.
I was simply overstimulated.

I've been able to explain clearly to my darling grandson why Grandma just can't take his teasing jump scare tricks or his sudden loud vocal tics. He knows that my nervous system is a delicate creature when it comes to noise.

Bless him, he really understands and honours my needs the best he can. He now saves his jump-scares for his Dad.

The discoveries were many as I worked out what triggered me and what soothed me. Music and dancing were the key to my regulation, along with good smells and sunshine on my face. I bought a diffuser and invested in some essential oils, really leaning towards honouring my senses. I bought a good, comfortable set of over ear headphones that I am barely seen without. No more big bright lights, lamps and twinkly LED lights were the way forward.

Who would've thought it would be the grief of losing my child that would ultimately lead to the discovery of my true self?

Now I understand what it is to come home. And there's no place like it.

Click my heels three times.
There's no place like home.
There's no place like home.
There's no place like home.

I vowed to myself were I ever to be in a romantic relationship again, I would not be cohabiting.

I value my space to be me. It's priceless. If I remain alone, that too is just fine.

Solitude is not a lonely state.

65

On Menopause and Ageing

Disclaimer.
These are my own personal thoughts and feelings about menopause. Every woman should do what they believe is best for themselves and their bodies with support from their doctor, therapist or spiritual healer.

When I turned 50, I was compelled to mark this half century of life achievement, so I threw a party that I grandly called my Croning Ceremony.

I invited friends and family to a small perfectly camp venue at a local pub, complete with a checker-board floor, red velvet curtains on a small stage and a huge glittering disco ball in the centre of the room.

David Lynch would've approved.

I almost expected Agent Dale Cooper and a short, backwards-speaking Man From Another Place to shimmy across the stage.

Ah! What a place to stage my transition into … What?

What was I actually doing? What was I celebrating?

Getting old? No, that wasn't it, being alive? Maybe, partly, it is a privilege to get old. After all, the alternative isn't great. I think I was just following some sort of guidance and making it up as I went along, hoping that the rationale and insight would get me into the doing of it all. I had a rough idea that at some point in the party I would get on stage, sit on a chair (call it a throne, perhaps?) and declare to all attending that I was about to enter the next phase of my womanhood. That was it. That was the full extent of the plan. I was just going to go wherever the flow took me.

My beautiful, creative performer friends really showed up for me. There were surreal cabaret style performances, latex striptease where no skin was ever revealed.

My darling Imogen memorably performed some of her original songs while my granddaughter did the 'holding hands and spinning around' dance with a small friend, the universal dance of all tiny people, it seems.

Good times were had as I marked this very significant shift in my life from Mother, to the Enchantress through to the Crone: the full complete woman.

I've never done things that I was supposed to as I've always followed my own inner compass. This explanation of the process of ageing into menopause, as being the full, complete woman, flew in the face of the current spirit of the times, surrounding this transition.

Documentaries on the television and news items informed me that once I entered menopause, I was broken, that the cessation of oestrogen production was a problem that needed resolving by supplementing with HRT.

Celebrities endorsed and promoted this concept, saying that if men went through this change, the fix would be put into place immediately.

Now, I'm not denying medical misogyny. There are all too many areas where women get a raw deal when it comes to debilitating conditions. Take endometriosis for instance, where women are gaslighted and left to suffer excruciating pain for years without proper diagnosis and treatment, but I believe that menopause is different.

Menopause evolved to save women's lives, not to damage them.

It is a natural, admittedly difficult process of evolving from one state of womanhood to another. I've heard it spoken of in terms of the second adolescence, and this makes a lot of sense. The dramatic and troubled shift from Maiden into Mother is reversed in menopause, when she then goes from Enchantress to Crone.

I believe that energetically, menopause is a shift into being, a spiritual passage, a becoming, a completing. The symptoms faced by women during Perimenopause are uncomfortable at least, and deadly at worst. Some women are plunged into depressions so severe that they risk taking their lives, so I don't take this lightly, if this feels like you, get help now!

Careful and diligent recording of mood states is always useful. A good therapist or body worker is recommended to be able to help process the rage that bubbles up from years of repressed anger that comes from living as a woman under Patriarchy. A good friend who is also going through it is invaluable. A problem shared is a problem halved.

Make friends with this rage, she is your guide through this turbulent time, your inner Medusa or KaliMa.

If at all possible, try to get to grips with any unresolved trauma before you enter this phase, if you do, you really help diminish the possibility of depression (which is simply rage turned inwards) setting in.

Shadow work is particularly useful to get into the dark corners of your psyche and dig out the hidden boogeymen. Dance! Move your body as much as you can. Shake to release stuck emotions. Let go, let go, let go and let go again.

Be mindful of the male gaze and it's tying into your validation. If you can still feel its seductive pull, place awareness there and gently, and compassionately, pull away from it, step by step.

Are you afraid of losing your libido? Have you noticed the lessening of its hold over your mind and body and felt that as a failure, of something wrong? Consider reframing this as freedom, releasing you from the tyranny of lust that can drive you to do the most unconscious things and leave you with the burden of guilt afterwards. Just because your libido is dropping doesn't mean you lose passion. Consider redirecting this passion towards creativity, a freeing up of space where you can focus on finding pleasure in doing the things you've always wanted to do, but never gave yourself the time and permission to do so.

It's your time now. So step into this portal of possibility.

What if I told you that hot flushes are a good thing? Anything that requires considerable change will be uncomfortable and intense. Just like contractions and surges of pain during childbirth, your hot flushes are doing wonderful, alchemical work.

My first experience of a flush was terrifying. I thought I was dying, no previous physical sensation had ever felt like this. It didn't feel hot, as such, even though the result was sweating. The closest I can get to explain to you this indescribable feeling, was a nuclear reaction inside my body, starting from my tail bone, (root chakra) and rising to the top of my head (crown chakra).

Now I understand this process as a burning through all the chakras, a potent energetic transformation.
Truly we are magnificent, magical creatures.

Understanding the flushes as something besides brokenness, and knowing that each power surge brought me closer to my complete woman, really helped me through them. That, and practical steps such as cooling mats and pillows to sleep on during the nighttime.

The phoenix rising out of the flames is a potent symbol of the burning through the dross of righteous rage.
You are ascending to the powerful and terrifyingly wise, self-loving, compassionate, mysterious goddess on earth that is your birthright as a woman.

Or you can take HRT and continue pleasing penises, there's fun in that too. Lord knows I've had my share.

I just prefer to be me now, even with the inevitable aches and pains that ageing brings, wrinkles, sagging skin, fatter belly, greying hair, failing eyesight, hearing loss and endless chin hairs that seem to appear overnight. Clearly, my crone self is manifesting physically.
The clarity of mind and focus back on the self that menopause eventually brings (after the brain fog of the chrysalis phase) due to the falling oestrogen levels, makes it all worthwhile.

I finally feel beautiful and whole. Even if the mirror reflects a different version based on societies warped beauty standards. Finally, I've made it home, back home to me, comfortable in my skin, in my body, at peace in my head, awed by my beautiful pattern seeking brain, and at peace with the world. I lean back into the mystery and sigh a deep sigh.

Everything was worth it.

Everything that brought me to this place was worth it.

What an incredible adventure it has been.

I'm 60 now.

My mother died at 65.

In a part of my mind, it has calculated that I'm running out of time.
I've also promised my granddaughter that I'd live until 106, so who knows what adventures still lie ahead?

All I know is that I'm not in control and nor do I want to be. I'm no longer afraid of death so I can live life intensely knowing I've got the best bunch of human ancestors waiting to hold my hand when it's my time to transmute and transform my final time.

But maybe that isn't the final time.

Who knows? I'm excited to find out either way.

Afterward

A Vibration Higher Than Love

Photo by Bari Goddard

I found it. I have finally worked out what I was meant to understand through this intrepid, chaotic, magical mystery tour called life. I've remembered for now, but am almost guaranteed to forget it. Such is the rhythm of life and the impact of the ego. I think we are meant to forget all the lessons we learn periodically through life to prevent us from becoming insufferable due to the fragility of our earthly egos. Only to remind ourselves later on, as if it was our very first discovery.

What have I found?

I've found my authentic self.

Finally, after the casting off of myriad masks, here I am.

Weird, awkward, magnificent, magical, messy and chaotic. Whole and perfect, in all of my imperfections. The closest to the God force that I have ever been. Best friends with my higher self and inner child.

Authenticity is the highest vibration of all.

It's hard won and potentially fickle. I'll keep reminding myself to come back to me the next time the storms roll in and I forget, yet again, that I am the blue sky. As for this moment, here I am.

AFTERWARD

www.ingramcontent.com/pod-product-compliance
Ingram Content Group UK Ltd.
Pitfield, Milton Keynes, MK11 3LW, UK
UKHW020751230625
6529UKWH00037B/750